INNOVATIVE RESOURCING

Empowering Rural Livelihood

Innovative Resourcing
Empowering Rural Livelihood

Edited by

I. Wanswett & D. Wanswett

SYNOD COLLEGE
Shillong - 793002, Meghalaya, India

AKANSHA PUBLISHING HOUSE
NEW DELHI • GUWAHATI • VISAKHAPATNAM

AKANSHA PUBLISHING HOUSE
4649-B/21, Ansari Road
Daryaganj, New Delhi-110002
Phones: 23268193, 09435116718
Email: ektabooks@yahoo.com
visit us: www.akanshapublishinghouse.com

Innovative Resourcing: Empowering Rural Livelihood

First Published 2011

ISBN 978-81-8370-271-3

PRINTED IN INDIA

Published by Akansha Publishing House, New Delhi-110002 and printed at Harmain Offset Printers, Delhi.

Contents

Acknowledgements

This Book would never have been accomplished without the encouragement and participation of many people. Our deep appreciation goes to each of the contributors for accepting the challenge of preparing the papers and sharing their ideas. To each we extend our sincerest thanks for a job well done.

We extend heartfelt thanks to all the participants of the National Seminar "**Innovative Resourcing: Empowering Rural Livelihood**" which was held in Synod College, Shillong, on the 15th - 16st October, 2009.

We are deeply grateful to Dr. D. Wanswett, the Principal of Synod College, Shillong whom without him this project would never have been possible. We appreciate his keen interest and participation to work tirelessly in making this Seminar a success.

We also extend our sincerest appreciation and thanks to Dr. M. Rani, the Coordinator IQAC, Synod College, and at the same time the coordinator of the Seminar, who has coordinated this seminar successfully. We also express a deep appreciation and gratefulness to Dr. D. Marngar who have extended his readiness in helping on the preparation of this book.

Finally, a very special note of appreciation to all the teachers of Synod College who kindly participated in making this task a success. We also thank the sponsoring agencies for their kind financial support, to all those who involved in this seminar and those who make this book possible.

Editors

Preface

India is a land of diversity with different types of terrain, various agro-climatic conditions, different levels of socio-economic conditions, and varied levels of regional development. India covers an area of 3,287,782 sq km and has a land frontier of about 15,200 km and coastline of about 6,000 km. The total population is about 1.15 billion. India has 70 per cent of its population residing in over 638,596 where villages, the goals to development consist of reducing poverty, raising levels of education, improving standards of health, enhancing empowerment and reversing the loss of environmental resources. About 260 million people in the country live below the poverty line, of these, 75 per cent live in the rural areas in villages. Known for its diversity, India accommodates about 25 percent of its population from indigenous and disadvantaged communities (Tribals and Dalits) known as scheduled tribes and scheduled castes. Agriculture is the mainstay of the Indian economy and contributes about 60 percent of the labour force; agriculture contributes nearly 26 percent of the GDP and accounts for about 18 percent share of the total value of the country's exports. The literacy rate in the country is 65 percent for males and 51 percent for females. The people in the rural areas live in extreme poverty as they are completely dependent on agriculture for their livelihood. Sadly, till today about 98% of the farmers belong to the small and marginal category where they are earning only a subsistence wage rate. As market oriented development approach proceeds, Indian rural farmers faces more disparity in income and this pushes them spiralling into a trap of vicious circle of poverty which continued with their coming generation.

Thus livelihood intervention is the key success for sustainability of people in the Indian rural economy. This can be done mainly by extending access and improving quality of public services including health, education and good governance.

The focus should be shifted on how to bring about a new change in the livelihoods of rural community and put them on the path of developmental processes.

This is a subject of great discussion among scholars all over India and the importance of rural development is seen by the priority given by the Central Government in terms of funds for the Ministry of Rural Development in facilitating development in rural areas of India and even in the North Eastern states.

In this connection, Synod College, Shillong after much thought and discussion has decided to conduct a National Seminar on the broad and thought provoking theme, "Innovative Resourcing: Empowering Rural Livelihood". Henceforth, the College invites public representatives, research scholars, academicians, resource persons to provide an in-depth analysis on these issues on the 15th- 16th October 2009 where Kum. Agatha K. Sangma, Union Minister of State, Ministry for Rural Development, Government of India inaugurated the Seminar as the Chief Guest. This book is the compilation of various papers, presentations and discussions of the Seminar of different scholars of the country.

I. Wanswett & D. Wanswett

Our Contributors

1. **A. Decruz**
   Managing Director, SoFMEDA, Shillong
2. **A.P.Warjri**
   Assistant Professor, Department of Geography, Synod College.
3. **Charles R. Lyngdoh**
   Assistant Professor, Department of Political Science, Synod College.
4. **D.D.Nengnong**
   Assistant Professor, Department of Geography, Raid Laban College.
5. **Dhiraj K. Borkotoky**
   Research Scholar, Department of Political Science, NEHU.
6. **D. Marngar**
   Assistant Professor, Department of Zoology, Synod College.
7. **I. Wanswett**
   Assistant Professor, Department of Economics, Synod College
8. **K. Nongrum**
   Assistant Professor, Department of Geography, Synod College.
9. **K.Rabha**
   Assistant Professor, Department of Zoology, Lady Keane College.
10. **Phrang Roy**
    Former President IFAD
11. **Pralay Kanungo**
    Professor, Jawaharlal Nehru University, New Delhi.

12. **Ratan Lal Godara**
Department of Economic Administration & Financial Management, University of Rajasthan, Jaipur.

13. **Shakira S. Islam**
Associate Professor, Department of Chemistry, Synod College.

14. **Shubhro Michael Gomes**
Assistant Professor, Department of Commerce, St. Xavier's College, Kolkata.

15. **Victoria Tauli Corpuz**
Chairperson, United Nations Forum on Indigenous Issues.

16. **W.R. Kharlukhi**
Associate Professor, Department of History, Synod College.

1

Indigenous People and Their Fundamental Rights on Environmental Protection and Development

Victoria Tauli Corpuz

All the indigenous peoples have the right to self determination and by virtue of that right they have the right to determine their political status and determine their economic social and cultural development. So, in the international law it has already been recognized that indigenous peoples have that right to be able to determine, decide and implement their own perspectives on how development should take place in their own communities. That is one article the Permanent forum is looking in to and the other one is Article 32 which is the article on the right to development which says that all the indigenous peoples have the right to determine their own development and they have their right to have a free and prior consent obtained before any development project is brought in to their communities. The principles that are enshrined in the UN Declaration on the Rights of the Indigenous Peoples, is the Declaration which the indigenous peoples have fought for the last 23 years until it got adopted in September 13, 2007. The main principles are to strengthen indigenous peoples as well as their cultures and identities, views and practices in terms of how development should take place in their own communities. This is very much appropriate for the theme that you are discussing now.

Challenges of Indigenous People at the Global Context

At the global context we are facing with three problems that we have never met before. In the year 2008-2009 we really faced tremendous global problems which require us to rethink how we are going to undertake development in our own local communities as well as in the whole world. There are three challenges or issues that we need to understand much better.

1. **The first issue is the problem of climate change**. Phrang Roy and I came from Bangkok on a two week meeting of the UN Framework Convention on Climate Change; the whole international communities' is negotiating on how to address this problem of climate change. The scientists of the intergovernmental panel on climate change in their fourth reports have come up with the conclusion saying that the climate change situations are already in a very critical stage. If we are not able to maintain and reduce the temperature of the world we are going to see more floods, more drought, or climatic events that are unprecedented; the melting of the glaciers of course is increasingly happening whether in the Himalayas or the glaciers in the Arctic. The glaciers are already melting in an unprecedented scale. If we are not really going to lower the green house emission we are really in deep trouble. That is what the scientists are saying and now it is up to the politicians to decide whether the international community is going to do something about these and decisively make policies and programmes that will lower our green house emission. The problem of climate change is a global problem and that not an individual national country can solve it but it has to be addressed by all the countries globally. Of course, the countries that need to do the most are the countries that contributed to the problems the most and these are countries like the United States which have only five percent of the total population of the world but contributed to eighty percent of the green house gas emission

in the atmosphere. Unfortunately in the last negotiation the United States did come up with the commitment of the targets they can reach. So we are in deep trouble if the United States and the European Union, the so called rich countries, are not going to do their responsibility in terms of cutting down the green house emission that they could do because of their industrialization, their transportation and of course their generation of energy. These things that are very much in the air and we don't know what is going to happen by the time the Copenhagen comes in December, 2009, where the agreement is supposed to conclude. This was one big problem that we are facing right now. The implication of this is that we have to adapt to the changes brought about by the climate change and adapting to this change, means that we have to do development in a totally different way. This is one of the challenges that we are going to face.

2. The second challenge is the massive erosion of the biological and cultural diversity. As you know bio-diversity is the source of food, fabric, foliage and everything that people need in the world and if this is eroding in an unprecedented scale then we will find ourselves in a situation where we have less species, food, medicine, animals and insect and the balance that is supposed to be there in the environment is skewed in a way that will disturb all the inter relationships that we see in the nature, not only between nature and man but in nature itself, i.e. between the different species. Along with erosion in the biological diversity there is the erosion in the cultural diversity and this is a big issue. With cultural erosion, many of the cultures in the world are going to disappear and all the bio- solutions, knowledge, thinking, views that are contributing to the heritage of knowledge of the world are going to disappear. This is happening massively among indigenous communities and among the remaining six thousand cultures and languages in the world, four thousands of these are found in indigenous communities. There is already massive erosion and disappearance of indigenous languages. The moment languages disappear, then the values, the culture, the knowledge disappear along with them.

3. **The economic crisis** in the United States has affected the world because, whether we like it or not, we are linked to the economy of this country. The economic crisis in the United States has tremendously affected the global market adversely affecting the livelihood of hundreds and thousands of people all over the world

These global problems have a huge impact on the indigenous peoples or tribal peoples in various parts of the world along with the people in Meghalaya as a part of it. One of the impacts is the increasing unpredictable climatic events that we see in different parts of the world. In the region from which I come from that is from the Philippines which has the same climate with that of Shillong with the same elevation and the same vegetation, we have had typhoons like never before. The recent Typhoons lasted in our communities for nine days causing massive landslides where around 300 people have died and majority of those who died are from mining communities because the communities have been totally mined out of gold, silver and copper. Tunnels have been dug under the earth and when the typhoons came causing massive landslide. Hundreds of houses collapsed and precious lives were lost. We never experienced anything like that. Even the floods that occurred in Manila are of the same case. We received rains in 6 hours which we normally get in one month. It fell continuously causing massive floods affecting not only the poor people but also the middle and upper class people of Manila because the divisions in which they are staying have been flooded. The floods are accompanied with diseases like malaria and dengue. These are the health problems that the Health Department in Manila cannot cope with. This problem is very much linked to climate change. Everyone is now concerned with climate change because it affects them directly.

The climate change and the unpredictable climatic events have brought about the problem of food security in Philippines. The paddy fields in islands in Philippines which are considered as the rice bowl of the country had been flooded and rice crop was destroyed and the country has to import rice to the amount of two billion dollars to be able to meet the food security of the people in the country. This is the situation that we faced and if you were there you would witness the impact of climate change.

In the Bangkok meeting two weeks ago we discussed extensively on how to undertake development in a totally different way because even seasons have changed. Normally, in Philippines typhoons stops in the month of September but now we are expecting typhoons in the month of October also. Earlier we have fifteen typhoons a year but now we have more than twenty five. This is a serious problem and people are thinking how to cope with the problem. We have to think what type of crops to plant to be able to cope with the floods and of course the droughts because after the floods we have long months of drought. This phenomenon is going to affect us further. There is food crisis and water crisis. This is the problem that we faced with. We have problem of diseases because of the heat. Incidence of malaria, dengue and other water borne diseases like cholera has increased. However, this only the tip of the ice-berg.

The issue now is first how to mitigate or to reduce the green house gas emission and how can we adapt and cope with these changes that are happening in our own community, what types of crops you need to develop, how do we address the issue of disasters, do we have the technology to meet the disasters, to predict them, do we have the capacity to address the issue of health due to the impact of these kinds of disasters. All these issues are entrenched to development strategy

Now in terms of the economic crisis that most of you are aware. The global crisis is caused by the liberalization of the financial market for they have loaned so much money to the people who cannot pay back, and when these people cannot pay back the loan to the bank that pay high salaries to the workers, these banks collapsed. The problem is with this crisis;

the rich countries that are affected have lowered or even stop contributing and fulfill their obligation towards development aid. If we are familiar with the Millennium Development Goals, it says that 0.7 percent of the national gross domestic product of the rich countries have to be contributed to the developing countries as aid, because this is their obligation to the developing countries. Because of the economic crisis they have enough reasons to say that they cannot contribute anymore which is so ironical, however, they are able to pay three trillion dollars to bail out the banks, the companies, the financial houses which went bankrupt, yet they say that they do not have the money to give for development aid. But first of all they don't even contribute to the climate change fund like the Adaptation Fund. As per the Convention Agreement and as in the Kyoto Protocol, that says it is the obligation of the rich countries that will have to lower and meet the green house gases emission by 40% by 2020 and by 90% by 2050 that they all agreed to. Another obligation is that they have to contribute finances to the developing countries because they have already occupied the atmospheric space and they polluted so much that the developing countries do not have much space to develop. They have already polluted 80% of the atmospheric space and only 20% is left and still they want to deprive the developing countries even this limited space available. This means depriving other developing counties for opportunity to develop. This is the main problem with the United States in relation to the developing countries like India and China. India and China rightfully said that it is only now that we are starting to develop and you deprive us that right to develop. Of course, the limit is set for the rich developed countries for green house gases emission because they have developed to the extent that they have already spilled out all the pollution to the atmosphere. The developing countries are saying you have to give us necessary finances to be able to mitigate or to lower green house gases emission. This is not the problem we created, but you created. You owe to pay us because you have polluted that space and you have to pay the taxes to us because you polluted the atmosphere and we cannot develop any more. They agreed on that and they are obliged to transfer technologies to us to develop pollution free technologies to reduce emissions from our cars, factories to develop our renewable energy sources so that we will not depend on coal, oil and gas which are the major causes of green house gas emission. You have to contribute to technology that will allow us to lower carbon emission and that will not contribute towards polluting the environment. These are the obligations but the developed countries are not meeting to any of them. They are not meeting towards mitigation fund; they are not contributing towards adaptation fund; and they are not lowering their targets. This is the big fight that is happening globally between the developed countries on the one hand and the developing countries on the other. The group of developing countries called the G-77 countries is pressuring the rich countries to meet their obligations. Unfortunately, the developed countries are not making any clear commitment that they will reduce the green house gas emission by 40%.

Sustainable Development and Protection of Environment

What do we have to do for rural development? First, rural development would mean that we have to go for the kind of development with low green house gas emission. This implies that we have to do development by depending on the renewable resources like solar, water and biomass. This is primarily because oil will be running out and the extensive use of it will contribute towards increasing the carbon dioxide concentration in the atmosphere. Second, rural development would mean development of our agriculture without depending much on petroleum based chemicals and fertilizers which contribute towards green house gas emission. Agriculture should be developed in a sustainable manner. The traditional agricultural practices of the indigenous people all over the world are very organic and sustainable. If the international community and the government support sustainable agricultural development, the productivity would be as much as the chemical and fertilized or industrialized based agriculture can produce. It should be remembered that sustainable agricultural products are even safer for the environment and the health of the people. That is one area that we have to seriously think about.

The other consideration is about soil management. One of the causes of green house gas emission is deforestation. The scientists have already established that 20% of the green house gas emissions is caused by deforestation and contributed mainly by the countries having the tropical rain forests. That is the reason why countries like Indonesia and Brazil have become the major polluters because of deforestation taking place in these countries. Many incentives are extended to many countries to stop deforestation. Countries or communities having more forests, more aids and incentives would be given to them to protect their forests. This is a good opportunity for indigenous people because they would be able to pressurize their government to respect their rights to have control over their own forests. The remaining forests in the world today are in fact found in indigenous people's territories and the reason for this is because we have followed our traditional forest management practices. Also, the indigenous people have asserted their claim over these forests and resisted the deforestation attempt by big forest companies or big plantation companies. So if we use this opportunity now to really call for reform in forest laws and forest policies, so that the rights of the indigenous peoples to control their forests and to continue their traditional forest management practice are respected. Through these efforts the territories and forest resources of the indigenous peoples would remain intact.

Another thrust of rural development is the food security and this assumes significance with the increasing occurrence of the unpredictable climatic events. There is a need to have crops that would be able to withstand floods and droughts. So the traditional knowledge of cultivation using the traditional crop varieties to suit the various climatic conditions should be encouraged. However, the problem is many of these traditional crop varieties are getting lost because of mono culture and green revolution. The challenge we have now is to rediscover the traditional knowledge of cultivation and to adapt to the problems of climatic changes.

Management of water resources is another issue for rural development. Water management is significant so that people can have adequate and safe water. There is a need to recover the traditional technologies. Indigenous peoples have developed their own technologies to manage water resources. Traditional technologies and knowledge need to be reinforced and learnt in schools as well as to be researched. Efforts have to be made to influence the government to use and encourage the traditional technologies not only for the survival of the indigenous peoples but for the survival of the nation and the whole world. The world is now looking to the indigenous peoples with their traditional knowledge to save the world.

2

Re -Thinking About the Future of Resourcing for Development

Phrang Roy

I joined the IAS in 1970. I was posted to Maharashtra and in 1975 I got my first charge of a district and the district was on the eastern side of Maharashtra where the rainfall is not very high where the topography allowed tanks to emerged and they would built tanks to used it for the water to percolates into the fields that was the form of irrigation system that traditionally has been built there. When I entered as the head of that district it was a year when Maharashtra went through three years of drought and it was in those three years that Maharashtra came up with what they then called the "Employment Guarantee Scheme" which now has been replicated nationally into the NREGA scheme that we have. So I was among the first of the young staff at that time who developed the Employment Guarantee Scheme work and in those period of three years the farmers had finished their seeds completely and we had to move in seeds from all parts of Maharashtra using all the abilities to do that. Then there was the question that since there is a potential for these low areas we need to make tanks under the Employment Guarantee Scheme as NREGA has done to create employment to the people but also to establish durable assets. What we found was we didn't have enough engineers to do the designing of these tanks but then I called a meeting of all the people and particularly the leaders of communities and we suggested that the engineer will give a talk to the people for two days on how to identify possible sites and the amazing thing was that 80 percent of what the people identified later the engineers verified that these were right. In one particular place it was a tribal area they knew that once it rains there would be no seeds and nothing would reached in because the area gets cuts out completely and trucks can no longer go there and the only way to do that was to ensure that the train service passes and the only train was the Howrah Mail but making the Howrah Mail stops in a small station was an impossible task. Thankfully at that time the IAS was still respected so we were able to tell the General Manager to halt the Howrah Mail and stop at the station and unload one of the wagons to do that and that in a sense to save that area or we would have had a scarcity for quite a long time. Now why am I saying this because when we look at resources I think there were a number of lessons that I learned from that. The first thing is that when you look at resources and try to mobilize them the important thing is to make sure that you have a delivery system and I think this point was highlighted yesterday in one of the presentations. The delivery was very important and in those days we have enough authority, we have enough confidence of the people that we were able to build that sort of delivery and I think it's very important that as we plan for resources we make sure that we have delivery. You cannot have delivery unless there is a governance system that gives you. There is a rule of law that there is a sense of responsibility of those who have to perform and of those who have to accept it. That was not just the official side it was also the political side. What was there in Maharashtra was that, even the politicians felt that they were responsible for development, they were held accountable by people for development and I think that helps in the growth that Maharashtra has seen over the years and over the reputation that it developed as a state that was progressive and that had results.

The second thing about resources is that sometimes you have to find resources in areas which we never thought about and when you look for resources for development it is not the most obvious ones the money and the others etc, but we found that for those tanks, we were able to built because we tried to tap the local knowledge of the local people and we found that actually designing a tank in a refining area was not rocket science it was something in which ordinary people could do if given the opportunities. So I think sometimes we need to demystify some of the scientific knowledge that we tend to pretend sometime in pursue of development and in the search for resources. I think it is very important that we also constantly look at opportunities to think out of the box as they say and to make sure that there are all scenarios that are taken into account. I was lucky in that year I was awarded by the Government of Maharashtra to be the best Performer Head of a district for the "Kharif Campaign" and after that I was immediately transferred to another district and because they said you perform so well you should go to another district which have more tribals, since you are a tribal and hence I was posted to Thana which is a district next to Bombay and has a very heavy industrialization and a very significant tribal population. It is one of those very unique districts of India. There I did not succeed. The kharif Campaign in the following year was not a success and what I found out was that when we were pushing very hard for High Yielding Variety seeds the tribal populations were very smart. They did not want to give up their low yielding seeds but they knew that they have to leave because the Government was as saying in India "Maa Baap" and to go against the Government means going against many of the benefits. They would take that seeds and grew it only in the lowlands but the food or the crops that they produced there they will not eat it. They will sell it to the market. Now one of the things that I found in this was the whole system of adaptation.

Vicky talked that with climate change we need to make adaptations but people are constantly making adaptations in their lives, adaptations to the vagaries of weather, adaptations to the vagaries of bureaucrats and governments approaches and I think it is a very important aspect when we look at resource mobilization that we take into account and one lesson that I learned from that was for people the most important item is food security and they will never never give up food security for income and this is one of the myths that we spread around in our development work. Lets raised the income of people, lets talk of income generation but income generation is secondary to the main concern of people and that is food security and so I think that was one of the lessons that I learned and there is a danger in resource mobilization and the attempts that we made to pushed our ideas so hard and when these ideas are created I mean very much part of the planning, the decision making at local, national and international levels and it frightens me when you look at how we made decisions. Decisions of three, four people we share a few ideas and we go "Wow this is a great idea, let's go" we get a government order, a cabinet decision it becomes God's Will and then we go about. Yesterday Vicky highlighted a point of "Free Prior and Inform Consent". I think when we do resource mobilization this is an extremely important point to remember. "Free Prior and Inform Consent" is a concept that has come in the last 2 to 3 years at the international dialogue we need to bring that down to our Governments. Is the work that we are doing in the Uranium Issue, its not whether its right or wrong but has there been a free, a prior and an inform consent? If I go to a doctor and I do a heart surgery and he tells me that the chances of you dying is at 10 percent will you still do this test and you says ok I'll take the chance the risk of 10 percent. Do we do that at the communities that we perform? We have an obligation that we have to do. That is a very important aspect.

I'd like to continue back to my story that from there I was transferred I suddenly got a call from the Deputy Chief Minister of Maharashtra who was a man, a Dalit but who had a major concern for indigenous or tribal people. He said Roy I have selected you to head "The Tribal Development

Corporation" so I said I have no idea of marketing, I've never been a student of marketing so how can I head He says no, since you are concern for the tribal peoples you go and in Maharashtra what you see among the tribal population is that middlemen take everything, so we came to the conclusion that middlemen were exploitative, so what we said we did and the concept of marketing was introduce, so it was state monopoly and Maharashtra was the first state to say that in the tribal areas nobody will purchased except from the Tribal Development Corporation. Overnight it became a huge operation and tribal populations used the extension services to say sell for you'll get income and it is very important. People start selling in huge amounts in other areas but the tribals sold in head loads which are not in huge amounts. Because of the pressure of not selling the rice which they were growing from the seeds provided by the government, they even start selling their own food security which affected them adversely and when we got the rice to be sold it was mixed together in various varieties and when it was sold in the market, it was at a loss because nobody would buy a variety of rice which has plenty of varieties and the whole thing became a disaster and I think but out of all that mistakes that we made in the system, I flourished because I was told that I was very committed to the tribal population as I was the head of High Yielding Varieties, etc and as a bureaucrat and as a development worker my future was very much built on the miseries of other people. That was a very hard lesson for me to learn and when I look back at that experience and looked at the development of the sixties and the seventies, It is not a mistake that I made but it is a mistake of the mindsets into which all of us were put into the development paradigm that was there and what was the development paradigm in the 60s and 70s which unfortunately continues in Meghalaya and others very strongly. Then if you talk to and I'm a member of the a State Planning Board and you discuss with people what is development, the answer would be that 80 percent of the people lives in agriculture, agriculture is the base so agriculture has a responsibility to mop out the resources, the capital, so with this capital then we can reached development, reached to industrialization and reached to happiness. That has been the model which economists have built over the 50s and 60s and because of that we developed a concept that maximization was very important. Let us maximized our production and we became obsessed with production, Let us produce let us have income to people because when they have income, we will have production then you will see growth, then you will see the well being of people to be improved. Unfortunately that has not proven for this very development paradigm which has led to a sort of economic crisis that the west faced in the last few years. Let us try and mop up colonization and under forces for our own good so that we can live in peace and therefore used resources. So this whole concept leads people who have done economics like me that maximization and profit making was an important aspect and I think some of the problems also which was explained yesterday on climate change and on economic crisis has come out of that. Now there were three major mistakes that we make in that process:-

1. We exaggerated that the government had the ability to coordinate all these activities but it is not the government only. Governments and technicians never understood the complex relationship between production, between the social, the environmental and the cultural dimensions. It is an aspect that we need to understand a little bit more carefully for example, we talk of food and food production and we fill up our houses but we tend to forget that people when it comes to festivals there is a particular kind of food that they will eat there which is a particular form of ritual that they will perform of which we don't take into account but in the minds of the ordinary people these are extremely important aspects. We talk of uniform knowledge systems. We are all brought up in the western knowledge system, we used the Cartesian approach, the logic and therefore even our analysis follows the reductionist approach of a logical framework the cause-effect relationship but there is another knowledge system, a

knowledge system that is more holistic, and a knowledge system of the indigenous people. They will grow twenty varieties in a small plot of land and anybody who is a student of logic will say that he must be the most idiotic person to do this but that is how nature does. There is a constant equilibrium in the different movement and that is how people have been experienced and this is a knowledge system which we have said as backward, underdeveloped etc. and we seldom see the stupidity into which we with modern knowledge are using. In the old system you will have your animals graze over the fields and there are two things that happen, the animals has fresh air and its wastes is then used to enrich the soil. What do we says that we are developed because someone will come with a commercial approach and put all the animals in one enclosure and what do we do with the waste that is now becomes a pollution by producing methane gas which messes up our climate and the soils. Is this the developed approach that we want to continue and I think even if we want to continue we will not be able to do that for the sake of everyone .The second thing is that when we look at food production and I think this comes particularly in the western world we look only at consumption, and if we look at transportation you'll find that the US genetically modified their tomatoes to be square so that when they transport it, it is much easier to transport and the cost can be brought down. We have brought down the cost of food production very low without taking into accounts the livelihoods of the people but worse without taking into account the issue of health. US today has such a huge problem in terms of health that yes they have cheap food but if you were to be sick in the US you will know how much you have to pay for your health and they don't have health insurance and that is what Obama is famous for.

I remember spending sometime in the Sonara desert in Arizona and there is a small group of Native Americans called the Ohdah about 10 thousand of them. These people live on the desert and live on beans. When you are in the desert and when you hit a tree it is like hitting a rubber cushion because all that moisture is kept on the tree and the beans and when they eat the beans water and nutrients are released very slowly and that is how they have survived and you don't need huge quantities but small amount that gives you energy to animals and people. In 1966, the Americans say that we must educate these native Americans, so they brought a typical American education from Kindergarten to Class 12. They opened a school, everyone claps their hands and say a great work done and they say that these poor native Americans must live like we do here, have mid day meals, so they give mid day meals with hamburgers in 1966 and by 1975, 66 percent of the population had diabetes which is one of the highest in the world. Why? Because they started eating up food in which their system could no longer absorbed, it went too fast that the sugar just build up on the system where as in the earlier days it was releasing energy quite frequently and these are things that we don't look at and so I think when you look at tribal population yesterday, Vicky has raised a point that land is such an important aspect. Our connection for land is more than just land in us. It is something spiritual something which Christianity never really understood in terms of the traditional religion that we have. The biodiversity that is there is something which is so important for us and the Kinship, the trust that we built. Today if you are in Europe, if you have a child what do you do, you say you have to go to work after three months and what do I do, I looked for someone I have to pay. I think its happening in Shillong too but in the older days you have another Kit or Kin to whom you pass on or you have 10 children, child number four will take care of that. So that the whole aspect has been broken and we have modified that by making it a commercial or a monetized aspect and then suddenly we says that we need resources to develop and what we have done earlier was completely ignored and I think this is something that we need to look at. Some of the traditional livelihoods we think that they are old fashioned but we have never looked closely. Shifting cultivation, only today that people have begin to understand that actually the system makes a lot of sense for biodiversity and for livelihoods, the system makes a lot of sense for climate change and its mitigation and I think we need to sort out and look back at some of these things and to realize in today's world especially for the rural areas. The rural communities are no longer the decision makers. The decision makers are the bureaucrats, the Governments policies makers and the international organizations. These are people who are deciding on behalf of the people what to do. That is one of the very basis in which some of the crisis in which we are facing today. For all this the Government is unable to cope, it is unable to make decisions. It is too complex and in our approach because of our thinking of a simplistic reductionist way, we will never be able to do that. That was the first mistake that we make and the first thing that we need to question is how we look into the future.

2. The second mistake that we've made is that we have underestimated the role of the private sector. When we said that we'll have the private sector we have this feeling of the unseen hands of the market. But when we are formed on the basis that I must make a profit two things happen; individualism becomes a driving force going very much against the collective aspects in which we have been born and brought up as a community and then what do you see when that happens, privatization takes place and when privatization takes place, it is not because of the Government but because of the choice that we make. You looked at the amount of landlessness among the Khasis in the last few years, Khasis may not be knowing that we have Ri Raid where everyone in the rural communities have some piece of land to be able to cultivate but all that is creating a problem and to make it worse at the higher level at the global level we are so keen on maximizing profits, we are so keen in terms of introducing our own profits that we produce more than what we have and then we go and dump that food somewhere else so that even that farmer cannot compete, and do you know that the tomato from Italy made in a tin, packed in a Tin shipped to Tanzania is cheaper than a tomato that a farmer can produced

in Africa and then we says a bloody, stupid African farmer he is so lazy he doesn't produce. Why should he produce when he can't sell? So I think that has been one of the big mistake and the new liberalism that has come over the market greed came in. What is the problem that has faced the US today? I have my children's friends 28 years old working in Britain, working in Hedge Funds London, have a bonus half a million dollars into their pockets, why because the bank pursue if you can bring in more and more profits by taking risk then we will start to pay you because they do make and the banking system is so much into speculation and so much taking risk that they brought down the whole institution, greed became the driving force and that greed will continue and we cannot allow that system to do. The third thing that we have made a mistake is that as part of that system earlier we used the "Farmers Organisation" and we broke them away. This is stupid, there's too much politics and theirs too much of Congress or NCP etc and because of that we say do away with all these sort of institution but we forget there are two or three things that are bad, some of these are cooperatives and farmers organizations that give a counter veiling force. They provide a space for people to discuss and dialogue. Those places are now being cramped up and now we are giving a solution of everything. So I think because of this I feel that the model that we have followed all these years is not a model that we can follow for sometime. Firstly I think that the world today is not as what it was at 70's, today the world faces climate change which will ask us that you will not be able to produce agriculture where 38 percent of green gas emission will take place. That green gas emission comes from fertilizers, pesticides and others. Secondly the price of petrol and the cheaper petrol will peak by the year 2040. You will not have enough of those resources. So continuing agriculture the way that we have done with fertilizers etc is not an option it will not be available. Meghalaya has an area where 42 percent of the areas are under forest we can say that our population is growing more than 2 percent. So one option which was available a few years was let's cut off the forest and grows more under agriculture. We will not be able to do that because when you do that you will lead to more problems with climate change. So we need to increase productivity, we will see that by 2015 atleast 18 percent of the population in the rural areas will move to the urban. There will be less people, who will produce, but we will have per capita to produce more but when we produce we have to fit in with the whole issue of climate change. We cannot just deforest areas as easily as we did before. What is that the problem? The issue that there is no simple solution. There will be different competing forces and trade off will take place. Trade off will be the sort of leading aspect of future thing. Nobody can come with a solution that this is the way. You just can't say organic agriculture is the answer, now can you say fertilizer is the answer, oil, environment will compete with each other for that limit space as Vicky says that in the atmosphere there is only 20 percent left and even within that 20 percent everyone is crowding in before the whole heaven will collapse on our head. So I think that is one thing that we need to do what do we need in the present, we need more consultations. These sorts of meetings are extremely important and I do not know the answer nor do you know the answer and I do not know what will happen 10 years, 20 years certainly within 50 years the whole equation will change completely. So when you are looking for resource mobilization for development the most important aspect is: i) consult each other , ii) acknowledge that there are different knowledge systems and that those people who are nearest to the ground probably know better than you and I who have learned from laboratories. We must come to recognize that there are two or three knowledge systems and to recognize that it means that we must change the system that we do research. We must change the Research work which we do. I mean if we look at all the Research works, we are looking at very small streams of specialization but we need to look a little bit closer into some of the areas but above all we need to have a rural focus. 80 percent of the population still lives in rural areas. I wanted for my own to find out how much of the Meghalaya budget is under the rural, so I consulted the Planning Department. They don't have the figures. In fact we have never broken a budget into rural and urban that was the reply that I got. I tried from the budget statements to see what it makes about my calculations in real terms and see that not more than 40 percent goes to rural areas and that too if you look very carefully below how you can do this when you say that 80 percent of the population is there. So I think the second change that we need to look in development is that we keep talking of this BPL (Below Poverty Line) we keep talking in Meghalaya about the poor. Personally I feel forget, I mean I work in an organisation that stood for the rural poor for 25 years. As the young chap within me, I forget that it's not the question. Don't look at your poor people as the poor who need your help. Look at them as they are the custodians of the knowledge that today you will need for your future existence under these new aspects. They are the guardians of our biodiversity. You knocked off your biodiversity you're gone. You can have your High Yielding Varieties of 10 tonnes as against the 1 ton produced by a person. You do that you will live 20 years less for a number of reasons. We need to look at them as the custodians, they know and I think we also need to look at now is what is being talked a lot more of the environmental services. The environment supports us with the neutral recycling, with the primary production. It provides us food, it provides fresh water and I think these are important aspects and sometimes now I want to save myself I take an "Aquaguard" but you say "No no no, Aquaguard is not good enough" I must have an RO reversible system. You can buy in Laitumkhrah these water systems that will clean off all the bacteria and then when we clean up the bacteria, we clean up all the minerals also then you have to take medicines to bring in minerals into your systems. We have become crazy, when I have that simple drinking water from a river side that flows, like it used to flow naturally. That is your best source that is a provision that we have. Flood Regulation is provided by nature and there's a certain regulation that the ecosystem does for climate change. When people grows certain things etc. they are just not doing it for growing, they look at the air and they know that there is a certain knowledge about that aspect and there is a cultural aspect. When Vicky's here, you say I want to take you to Cherrapunjee because you are proud of your landscape. You are proud of the aesthetic sense. You take your bag if your weaving is lovely as this comes from your area. So these are the services and we need to support those who are being the custodians. Yes production will be required and we can look at organic and looked at it as a possible way of doing this but I think you also need to look into the issue not just of production but the processes. Yesterday with due respect Toki showed us about the cauliflower and that was a very important production but what about the process, Do you want the process to be produced only by one person who becomes rich or do you want the process to be one where all small farmers have a role to play and if you look at production only from production and forget the process, the process of distribution, etc. we will land ourselves into great difficulties.

3. The last point is the issue that we need resources because of vulnerability. One aspect that we have to take into account is that increasingly we will have economic shocks; people who have made profits of 1 million, 2 million, and 500 millions will not give up. This fanatic system will continue with a few tinkering here and there. But those systems will make us much more, people who will be getting in shocks, and we will be seeing more and more of that. We will have climate change and we will have disasters. These will come our way and the state has a responsibility to ensure that our vulnerability to these aspects particularly that of the small and the poor are protected and are you prepared if there's a drought here; are you prepared if there's an earthquake; are you prepared if there is flood in certain areas? What has the state done into this thing; what provisions have been made; what resources have we done into this? Resources that is both knowledge and resources in terms of goods and services that will be supplied. I think these are the aspects that are

very important. This is where we must be asking the state to move not in decision making on those matters where poor people affect their lives. We must recognize the poor person, the rural person, the individual and the collectors to be the centre of the decision making. We must become co-workers with them in creating, in research, in the knowledge systems that we built but we must not forget the state has a role to play when we are vulnerable otherwise we don't need a state, why create a state if it cannot defend my things and lastly we cannot have this unless we are free from the security problems. My personal security and your personal security are important. If a state cannot make me live in a secure sense it is not worth having a state, the state is not meant to go with red lights protecting a few people. The state is meant to protect the personal safety of everyone and that is where I would put my resources and that is important and the security I need is the security of tenure, security of access to resources that can give me the livelihood without that I will not. As I said security from disasters, disasters that have become man made and which are made by us. So I feel when you look at all these issues, it cannot be business as usual, you just cannot go to your state, to your Planning Board etc. and says well lets allocate money; its much deeper and there I think the communities and people have to be involve because they will be affected and they must know before it affects me what is there and to do that in a non violent, to do that in a consultative way and to do that in an inclusive way. It is not only the poor who must be there, only the rich must be there, but we must all be there. But we are there not just as stakeholders but as Right holders, people who have rights in all these issues. Only then we can have a development but I think as an academic institution I think you need to rethink completely what you have learned and what you are teaching and I think these seminars are the beginning of that process so that we can rethink, we can relook what I did and what I studied should not be what you did and what you study. Your world is a very different world than what I've seen and I hope it will be a better world.

3

Animal Rearing an Innovation to Poverty Alleviation in Rural Meghalaya

D. Marngar & I. Wanswett

Introduction

The Meghalayan food comprises of rice along with fish or meat preparations. In fact, rice is the staple food of the people of Meghalaya.

It can be said that the people of Meghalaya have a very liberal food habit from rice to maize, millet, tapioca, etc. Besides, the people of Meghalaya rear goats, pig, ducks, fowls and cattle for their meat. Furthermore, the inhabitants also eat the meat of bison, deer, wild pigs, etc. Fish, crabs, eels, prawns; dry fishes also form a major part of the food in Meghalaya.

Thus, it is evident that the Meghalayan food is a typical Meghalaya cuisine with its own innovations and delicacies.

About 80 - 85 % of the total human population in Meghalaya consumes meat. The availability of productive animals (cattle) is less and as such the demands of beef can not meet by the people. The focus, as a result, is to increase more cattle production, pigs and goats to produce more meat and extra income from these animals.[1]

The huge gap between production and consumption of meat in terms of quantity in Meghalaya has manifested the huge investment potentials for the rural population in cattle rearing and poultry business.

Meghalaya imported around 9,930 metric tonnes of meat from mainland India to cater to the demand of 36,690 tonnes in 2007-2008. In 2006-2007, it was 11,152 metric tonnes. The domestic production of meat was 26,760 tonnes in 2007-08 and to meet the shortfall, the State imported 8,914 metric tonnes of cattle and buffaloes (beef), 966 metric tonnes of pork and 50 metric tonnes of mutton.[2, 3]

In 2006-2007, 9670 metric tonnes of beef, 9996 metric tonnes of pork and 1,030 metric tonnes of mutton and 3979 tonnes of chicken were imported. Although the statistics revealed the huge potential of piggery, poultry and cattle rearing in the State, people are not forthcoming.[2, 3]

"The problems of bank loans, demand for mortgage, long formalities expensive feeds are the main reasons that stop the poor rural population from exploiting the opportunities," said the Director of Veterinary and Animal Husbandry Department of Meghalaya. The official, however, said there were a couple of new schemes that could attract the people to start their venture in a lower scale. Meghalaya's consumption of fish is more than what it produces. It produces 6,000 metric tonnes of fish annually whereas the demand is 11,000 metric tonnes.[3]

Method of Study

The study was conducted by direct interview with the local people (farmers), meat sellers and the butchers themselves in different places (12 places) of Meghalaya. Questionnaires were also prepared and were provided to them for their responses. Based on these studies, statistical analysis was conducted using One Way ANOVA.

Results

Due to its peculiar topography and economy the people of Meghalaya need to depend more on the sectors like Animal Husbandry, Horticulture etc. as compared to traditional Agriculture. To bring about a developmental change in livestock and dairy sector, number of programs and infrastructure development are undertaken where the activities are mainly centered around the following broad objectives: -

* Providing protection to livestock and poultry from the ravages of *diseases* through treatments and preventive vaccinations.
* Introducing improved breeding techniques for upgrading the local stock.
* Ensuring better Animal Husbandry practices through adoption of Extension and Research.
* Building up of adequate technical and professional man-power through Education and Training.
* Encouraging setting of Livestock and dairy Industries.

The then Chief Minister of Meghalaya Shri Donkupar Roy said poultry and livestock is an integral part of agriculture and contribute significantly towards uplift of the rural economy as well as generate employment opportunities for the rural population.[4]

The Chief Minister informed that the State has many small farms with minimum production and there is a big gap in understanding their problems. Therefore, he also stressed on the need to applying some kind of remedies while making programmes and policies in favour of small farms for higher production and sustainability. The main objective of the National Project on Cattle and Buffalo breeding is to improve the indigenous cattle and buffalo in respect of their productivity and cost efficiency and to increase income of the farmers.[4]

In our studies to find out the consumption rate of pork (pigs), beef (cows), mutton (goats and sheep) and chicken in 12 places of Meghalaya. The following tables show the detailed results.

Table 1. Consumption of animals for meat /day in 12 places of Meghalaya

City/Town/Village	*No. of Pig/day*	*No. of Cow/day*	*No. of Goat/day*	*No. of Chicken/ day*
Jowai	40	36	03	400
Polo Market	06	06	10	200 300
Mairang	08	12		180
Mawkyrwat	03	08		50
Phudmawrie	10	10		80
Iewduh	140	36	22	800 1000
Tura	09	08	25	100
Sohra	10	6	1	10
Nongpoh	7	10	3	15
Mawsynram	1.5	0.5		5
Tyrsad	3	0.5		5
Borsora	1	0.5		5
	239	**129**	**64**	**3150**

The table above showed the detailed consumption of animals (meat) in the 12 places of Meghalaya. Iewduh in Shillong was found to be the highest consumer of animals for meat compared to other places.

Mutton (Goats) consumption is less compared to that of pork and beef in rural Meghalaya, but the consumption of mutton is more in urban areas of Meghalaya. Iewduh and Tura markets consumed mutton the maximum of about 22 and 25 numbers per day respectively (Table 1).

In the study we found that the average cost of a pig is Rs 7000/-, a cow is Rs 10,000/-, a goat is Rs 5000/-, and a chicken in general is Rs 250/-. The average weight of a pig is 55kg, a cow is 85kg, a goat is 45kg and chicken is 1.5kg. The total amount of money spent in animals per day, the total amount of money that spent outside the state for purchasing animals and the amount of money that spent within the state for purchasing animals in these 12 places are given in Table 2.

Table 2. Total Amount of money (Rs) spent in Cow (Beef), Pig (Pork), Goat (Mutton) and Chicken per day in 12 places in Meghalaya

Item	*Total No. of animals/ day*	*Cost/ animal in Rs*	*Total amt/day (Rs)*	*Total amt (Rs) Spent outside the state/day*	*Total amt. (Rs) remained in the state/day*
Pigs	239	7000/-	16,73,000/-	13,25,800/-	3,47,200/-
Cows	129	10,000/-	13,35,000/-	12,14,000/-	1,21,000/-
Goats	64	5000/-	3,20,000/-	1,55,000/-	1,65,000/-
Chicken	3150	250/-	7,22,500/-	-	7,22,500/-
Total	3572		40,50,500/-	26,94,800/-	13,55,700/-

In general the amount of money spent in cows, pigs, goats and chicken in 12 places of Meghalaya per day is Rs 40,50,500/- and Rs 26,94,800/ of money has gone outside the state in purchasing the animals, whereas only Rs 13,55,700/- of the total amount remained within the state for purchasing these animals.

In the markets the cost of pork is Rs 160 /kg, beef is Rs 120/kg, mutton is 200/kg and chicken is 250 / Number taken in general both local and broiler respectively (Table 3) in 2009. Considering in term of Kg of meat in all 12 places about 31,710 kg of meat are consumed per day at the cost of Rs 51, 76, 250/-. Comparing the total amount of money in term of total cost in kg of meat and that of total number of animal, there was a benefit of 28%. This indicates that the butchers gained a handsome of benefits from selling meat in the markets which becomes one of the good businesses for earning a livelihood.

Table 3. Total amount of meat consumed per day in kg and the amount of money spent per day in meat in 12 places of Meghalaya

Items	*Ave. Amt of Kg/ day (Rs)*	*Rate (Rs)/Kg*	*Total Amt of money/day (Rs)*
Pork	239 x 55 = 13,145	160	21,03,200/-
Beef	129 x 85 = 10,965	120	13,15,800/-
Mutton	64 x 45 = 2880	200	5,76,000
Chicken	3150 x 1.5 = 4720	250	11,81,250
Total amount in Kg (3572 No.) 31,710 kg			**51, 76, 250/-**
Amount of money in term of Total Nos. of animals			40,50,500/-
Benefit (28%)			**11, 25, 750/-**

Table 4. Total Amount of money (Rs) spent in Cow (Beef), Pig (Pork), Goat (Mutton) and Chicken in a week, in a month and in a year in 12 places in Meghalaya

Item	*Total No. of animal/ week*	*Total Amt. of money/ week (Rs)*	*Total amt of money/ month (Rs)*	*Total amt of money/ year (Rs)*
Pigs	1434	1,00,38,000/-	5,01,90,000/-	61,06,45,000/-
Cows	774	77,40,000/-	3,87,00,000/-	47,08,50,000/-
Goats	384	19,20,000/-	96,00,000/-	11,68,00,000/-
Chicken	18,900	47,25,000/-	2,36,25,000/-	28,74,37,500/-
Total		2,44,23,000/-	12,21,15,000/-	148,57,32,500/-

The total amount of money spent in meat in the 12 places which was expressed in term of one week, one month and one year are shown in table 4 above.

Table 5. Total amount of money (Rs) that spent outside the state in buying these items

Items	*Amt of money spent outside day (Rs)*	*Amt of money spent outside/ week (Rs)*	*Amt of money spent outside / month (Rs)*	*Amt of money spent outside/ year (Rs)*
Pigs	13,25,800/-	79,54,800/-	3,97,74,000/-	48,39,17,000/-
Cows	12,14,000/-	72,84,000/-	3,64,20,000/-	44,31,10,000/-
Goats	1,55,000/-	9,30,000/-	46,50,000/-	5,65,75,000/-
Chicken				
Total (Rs)	26,94,800/-	1,61,68,800/-	8,08,44,000/-	98,36,02,000/-

The above table showed the amount of money spent outside the state in purchasing animals in a week, in a month and in a year respectively.

Table 6. Total amount of money (Rs) that remained in the state in buying the following items

Items	*Amt of money remained in the state/ day (Rs)*	*Amt of money remained in the state/ week (Rs)*	*Amt of money remained in the state/ month (Rs)*	*Amt of money remained in state/ the year (Rs)*
Pigs	3,47,200/-	20,83,200/-	1,04,16,000/-	12,67,28,000/-
Cows	1,21,000/-	7,26,000/-	36,30,000/-	4,41,65,000/-
Goats	1,65,000/-	9,90,000/-	49,50,000/-	6,02,25,000/-
Chicken	7,22,500/-	43,35,000/-	2,16,75,000/-	26,37,12,500/-
Total (Rs)	13,55,700/-	81,34,200/-	4,06,71,000/-	49,48,30,500/-

Table above indicated the amount of money that spent within the state in purchasing animals for food which was expressed in a week, month and year respectively.

Table 7. Total amount of Money (Rs) that spent for meat (in No. of animals) in 12 places of Meghalaya

Items	*Total Amt ofmoney/ day (Rs)*	*Total Amt of money/ week (Rs)*	*Total Amt of money/ month (Rs)*	*Total Amt of money/ year (Rs)*
Meat	40,50,500/-	2,44,23,000/-	12,21,15,000/-	148,57,32,500/-
Total amount of money spent outside the State				98,36,02,000/- (66%)
Total amount of money remained in the State				49,48,30,500/- (34%)

Thus, the state has loss 66% of the total amount of money a year in purchasing animals from other states of India and only 34% of the total money was spent within the state in buying these animals (Table 7). Hence, there is an urgent need for the people of the state to realize the importance and benefit of rearing and culture these animals in our own state in order that this huge amount of money would not go outside the state every year and thus would generate employment especially in the rural areas, and to enhance the rural economy and overall economy of the state.

Animals forms a part of the village economy for meat, milk and to a lesser extent manure. Of the four species relevant to leather industry, cattle and goats are prominent in Meghalaya. Between these two also, cattle is a predominant source of meat for local population. Goats are raised mainly as a source of supplementary income by selling them to the nearby towns where there is a demand for goat meat. Nepali migrants introduce buffaloes, of late, in the state. In the case of sheep, as there is no demand for meat, their rearing is very insignificant. However, pigs are raised widely in backyards of residences and their meat is consumed along with skin.

In terms of density of livestock, Meghalaya falls well below the national average, but their ratio to human population appear significant. West Garo Hills district possesses high concentration of livestock among the seven districts of the state.[5]

Table 8. Availability of hides and skins in Meghalaya from the source of slaughter houses in a year

Item	*Number of hides/ year*	*Rate/ hide (Rs)*	*Total amt. of money Rs./year*	*No. of wastage of hides/year*	*Amt. of money lost by wastage of hides/ year*
Cattle hides	2,55,000	500/-	12,75,00,000/-	84,000	4,20,00,000/-
Buffalo hides	2000	700/-	14,00,000/-	-	-
Goat skins	2,05,000	300/-	6,15,00,000/-	29,000	87,00,000/-
	Total		19,04,00,000/- +		5,07,00,000/- Recovery rate @
7%					
			+35,49,000/-		=35,49,000/-
Total	4,62,000		19,39,49,000/-		4,71,51,000/-

Hides and Skins

Hides from cattle and buffalo, skins from goats and sheep are generally sourced from slaughter houses. In view of the non-existence of traditional flayers in Meghalaya, almost all fallen animals are being buried resulting to

The annual wastage of around 84,000 hides and 29,000 skins

The value of such loss accounts about Rs.4 crores annually

The value of recovery hardly works out 7% of the total assumed value of fallen hides in the state.

Availability of hide and skin in Meghalaya from the source of slaughter is shown in Table 8.

Important markets for hides and skins

There are two important markets viz. Shillong and Tura for raw hides and skins in Meghalaya. The trading with other parts of country takes place only through Shillong and Tura markets. The important characteristics of the markets have been discussed below.

Shillong

Shillong has been the major base, especially for good quality hides in the whole of North East region which gets supplies from Khasi and Jaintia Hills. There are four major feeding centres for Shillong. They are Jowai, Mairang, Nongstoin, and Nongpoh.

In addition, there are number of weekly markets held throughout the year in various parts of Khasi and Jaintia Hills and supplies from these markets flow into Shillong market.

The average weekly transactions in Shillong for animal hides accounts to 4200 cattle hides, 50 buffalo hides and 1400 goat skins.

About 50% of the hides are in the weight range of above 16 kg.

On an average 70% of the cattle hides are graded as of good quality.

About 30% of the local arrivals into Shillong market illegally move to Bangladesh, especially cattle hides in the weight range of 12-16 kg.

Within the country Kolkata is the prominent destination followed by Chennai.

Tura

It is the second biggest market in Meghalaya. The supplies feed the Tura market from the whole of Garo Hills region comprising East Garo, West Garo and South Garo Hills districts. Hides and skins are sourced from number of weekly markets as well as from regular slaughter in major villages and towns. Except the supplies from Tura town, other sources are not found to be major ones.

Table 9. Average availability of hides/week from the following centers is as follows:-

Centre	*Items*	*Availability in No.*	*Rate/ No.*	*Amount of money (Rs)*	*Total*
Jowai	Cattle hides	450	500	2,25,000/-	
	Buf. hides	35	700	24,500/-	2,94,500/-
	Goat skins	150	300	45,000/-	
Mairang	Cattle hides	300	500	1,50,000/-	1,50,000/-
Nongstoin	Cattle hides	200	500	1,00,000/-	1,00,000/-
Nongpoh	Cattle hides	50	500	25,000/-	
	Buf. Hides	10	700	7,000/-	
	Goat skins	25	300	7,500/-	39,500/-
Shillong	Cattle hides	900	500	4,50,000/-	
	Buff. Hides	50	700	35,000/-	
	Goat skins	500	300	1,50,000/-	6,35,000/-
Williamnagar	Cattle hides	40	500	20,000/-	
	Goat skins	35	300	10,500/-	30,500/-
Kherapara	Cattle	25	500	12,500/-	12,500/-
Baghmara	Cattle hides	20	500	10,000/-	
	Goat skins	25	300	7,500/-	17,500/-
Tura	Cattle hides	250	500	1,25,000/-	
	Goat skins	135	300	40,500/-	1,65,500/-
				Total	14,45,000/-

The markets get weekly 250-500 cattle hides, 135- 450 pieces of goatskins and sheep skins (Table 9).

About 55% of the total arrivals of cattle hides are in the weight range of 8-12 kg. Though Calcutta and Guwahati are major destinations, occasionally supplies move to Bangladesh through illegal trade[5].

Industries related to Cattle Products

Tanning

Tanning industry is the backbone of leather related activities. There has been no historical record of traditional tanning industry in Meghalaya.

Leather Products Industry in Meghalaya

Although all type of leather products is widely used in the state, there are no traditional leather products manufacturing industry in Meghalaya. As demand for modern footwear has grown due to urbanization of the state, it is leading to migration of traditional artisans from Uttar Pradesh, Bihar and West Bengal into Shillong and Tura regions. There are also few Chinese artisans who have been operating in Shillong for last few decades who have established a niche in the footwear market over the period of time. There is a booming market for all types of footwear in Shillong since the climate is very subtle throughout the year in Khasi & Jaintia Hills. Further, the local people have a fancy for variety of fashionable footwear.[6]

Footwear Manufacturing in Meghalaya

Apart from Shillong, there are number of traditional artisans in Tura but most of them have confined themselves to the repairing work. In addition, a few local individuals who got trained in this line have also established their own units in various parts of the state. However, the impact of these units is not significant. There are altogether 27 footwear manufacturing units in Shillong which employ about 110 workers. These units manufacture both leather and non-leather footwear. Only five units predominantly manufacture non-leather footwear.[5, 6]

Marketing

It is estimated that there are nearly 150 footwear retail shops in and around Shillong. On an average each shop sells 80 – 100 pairs per day during the peak season and 40-50 pairs during lean season. The sale of footwear during peak season (i.e., winter) works out 15 lakh pairs and during lean season 11 lakh pairs aggregating 26 lakh pairs of footwear in Khasi and Jaintia Hills. On the other hand in Garo Hills, except Tura all the other markets are largely rural. Altogether an estimated 60 – 65 lakh pairs of footwear are sold in Meghalaya state annually. Of this approximately 15 lakh pairs do purely leather footwear and the rest comprise mixed leather and non-leather footwear.[5, 6]

As regards to the local supplies of footwear from the manufacturing units in Shillong, such production accounts hardly 5% of total footwear sold in Shillong. The annual production from local makers works out about 1.5 lakh pairs per annum.

Total Amount of money spent in footwear/year is

60 lakhs pairs x Rs 200/pair = Rs. 120,00,00,000/-

Total Amount that generated locally/year is

1.5 lakhs pairs x Rs 200/pair = Rs. 3,00,00,000/-

(Taken the minimum cost of footwear per pair)

Total Amount of money that spent for importing footwear/year is

Rs. 117,00,00,000/-

Marketing of Leather Garments

The consumption of leather garments in India is very limited and largely confined to the higher altitude places like Shillong. The market of leather garments is fairly good in Khasi and Jaintia Hills and almost all the sales take place from Shillong market. On the other hand, there is no significant market in Garo Hills.

Field information reveals that altogether 80-100 garments are sold per day during peak season i.e., the Christmas season. During the rest of the year around 20 garments are sold per day. In other words, annual sales account about 15000 garments in Shillong market. Of this, the proportion of premium segment is around 15%.[5, 6]

Marketing of Leather Goods in Meghalaya

Leather goods comprising handbags, wallets, cases, gloves are the major consumer items being exported from India. Consumption within the country is very limited and confined to gift articles for corporate business groups. Incase of Meghalaya, the market for leather goods exist in Shillong town, being cosmopolitan in nature. The peak season for sales is Christmas period. On an average 18,000 – 20,000 leather articles particularly hand bags are sold during peak season in Shillong market. The annual transactions of leather goods account 42,000 – 45,000 pieces.[5, 6]

Conclusion

In completion of the study in the 12 places in Meghalaya it was found that 3456 numbers of animals and 19,730 kg of meat were consumed per day generating a huge amount of money. The results have shown that a larger amount of money in purchasing animals has gone outside the state since the production of animals within the state is not sufficient to meet the demand in the markets. On seeing these results, there are a lot of scopes for the rural people of Meghalaya for cattle farming, piggery, and poultry to produce these animals and meet the demands in the markets in the state. This business would help rural people from unemployment, eradicate poverty, increase rural economy and also increase the economy of the state as a whole[8].

In these few years there is an increase in the domestic production of animals in the rural areas. Though the Govt. has encouraged people to take up this job, but the problems came up with the banks.

At present some banks like NABARD has taken initiatives to enhance the animal farming in the rural areas of Meghalaya.

In its "India Livestock and Products Annual 2008", USDA said both poultry and buffalo meat have "no specific religious sentiments attached" to their consumption. However, the US body quoting Census of India also said Hindus who comprises around 80 per cent of the total population do not consume beef, while 13 per cent Muslims do not eat pork. "Nevertheless, the younger generation is changing their food habits to non-vegetarian and other processed foods. Consequently, with rising income levels, domestic meat consumption has the potential to rise further," it noted.[7]

Buffalo and poultry meat is popular in India because of their price competitiveness, it added. Beef consumption is forecast to increase by five per cent to 1.94 million tons during 2009 from the previous year. The report also said per capita beef consumption is estimated at 1.6 kg compared to 1.8 kg for poultry meat. "Beef consumption continues to rise as it remains the cheapest of all the meats available in the domestic market," it said. The per capita meat consumption in India is estimated at 5.5 kg per year, which is much lower than 10.8 kg per year as recommended by the Indian Council of Medical Research (ICMR), USDA said.

So dear friends go ahead for cattle rearing in Meghalaya, which will bring happy days for the animal rearing farmers in the state.[7]

REFERENCES

1. Rural populace yet to tap State marketing cattle rearing and poultry business. Mawphor. Saturday July 18, 2009
2. Prospects of piggery, poultry bright in Meghalaya: *Sentinel*, July, 17, 2009
3. *Eastern Mirror* – Nagaland, Shillong,: July 17, 2009
4. Chief Minister lays stress on livestock farming The Shillong Times: 11th July 2008.
5. Leather & Allied Industries in Meghalaya NEDFi Databank Monday, 19/01/2009
6. *Economic Survey on Leather And Allied Industries in Meghalaya.* Meghalaya Industrial Development Finance Corporation Limited, August, 1997
7. Meat Cattle Rearing – A Boooon !!!!. Agricultureinformation.com 09-10-2008
8. Animal Husbandary and Veterinary: NEDFi DATABANK, Wed, 12/10/2008

4

Rural Marketing in Meghalaya-A New Mantra

I. Wanswett

The development of the nation largely depends on the development of the rural population. About 75 percent of the total population in India resides in the rural areas; most of them live below the poverty line. In order to develop the rural areas, apart from the basic facilities like health care and education, the mindset of the people should be changed with a focus on marketing in order to enhance their skills and knowledge. This would increase their competitiveness in exploiting their resources and increasing their income level. Rural marketing is a new venture undertaken by companies launching their products in the rural market with strategies relative to a rural consumer.

Rural Marketing - Definition

Prime Minister Dr. Manmohan Singh talked about his vision of rural India: 'My vision of rural India is of a modern, agrarian, industrial and services economy co- existing side by side where people can live in well-equipped villages and commute easily to work, be it on the farm or non-farm economy. There is much that modern science and technology can do to realize this vision. Rural incomes have to be increased. Rural infrastructure has to be improved. Rural health and educational needs have to be met. Employment opportunities have to be created in the rural areas'.

There has been a tremendous socio-economic change in the rural areas. 'Go Rural' is a slogan which is used by marketing gurus and entrepreneurs and thus rural marketing emerged.

Rural marketing is often confused with marketing of agricultural products but basically it means penetration of a market in the rural areas.

Thus we can define rural marketing as the promotion of a company's products in the rural markets by using strategies which differ from those of the urban market because a rural consumer is more price sensitive but not to the quality of a good.

Concept of Rural Marketing

The concept of rural marketing has played an important and influential role in the lives of people living in the rural areas. In India most of the districts and towns are connected with the rural markets. The rural population is three times that of the urban areas and rural consumers are now the prime targets of various durable and non-durable products, food, telecom services besides hundred percent agricultural inputs such as seeds, fertilizers, pesticides and farm machinery. The rural population in India accounts for around 627 million, which is exactly 74.3 percent of the total population.

A rural market represents those segments of overall market of any economy which is distinct from other kinds of markets and they constitute an important segment of the economy with a definite population. Typically, a rural market will represent a community in a rural area with a population of 2500 to 30000.

Rural marketing in Indian economy has been in three kinds of marketing framework:

1. Rural to Urban transactions

These mainly include agricultural products like food grains, oilseeds, cotton, potatoes, produce by rural industries that finds a market in the urban areas.

2. Rural to Rural transactions

Here production and consumption of goods are mainly confined to rural areas.

3. Urban to Rural Flow

It is the flow of manufactured goods namely consumables, durables, services etc. It also includes marketing for agricultural inputs like fertilizers, pesticides, seeds and so on.

The concept of rural marketing in India is always considered to be in ambiguity because people are often confused that rural marketing is agricultural marketing – the latter denotes marketing of agricultural products to urban areas whereas rural marketing involves marketing of manufactured products or services to rural consumers and rural producers or in other words, rural marketing means carrying out business activities by the flow of goods from urban to rural regions of the country.

However, rural markets are growing and are in a progressive sequence with more income being generated from the rural areas.

Importance of Rural Marketing

In recent years, rural markets have acquired a great significance in countries like India and China where vast majority of the population resides in the rural areas. Its importance is seen in the overall growth of the economy which has resulted in a substantial increase in the purchasing power in the rural communities. With the success of the 'Green Revolution' agricultural productivity has increase which has resulted in an increase in the income level of the rural consumers. The rural India has a high purchasing power and the rural community is often considered as a 'sleeping giant' because of its vast untapped resources waiting to be tapped. Rural consumers spend around 13 percent of their income, the second highest after food (35 percent) on fast moving consumer goods (FCMG) as per a RMAI study. While there is large growth in the urban market, the rural or latent market is yet to be tapped which has enormous resources for growth. Rural market is gaining importance because the urban market has become saturated for the marketing gurus. Most of the marketers in the urban market have been targeted and due to stiff competition in the urban market companies try to venture to the unexplored region i.e. the rural areas. Driving the growth are categories like telecom, IT and insurance. Players including AirTel, Vodafone, Nokia, HDFC life amongst others are spending considerable amount of investment in taking their products and services to smaller towns and villages. Primarily, it's the well established like Amul, Mahindra tractors that have the benefits of rural marketing. Others are realizing the potential of rural consumers and are ready to invest big bucks for being a success in the rural areas. Hindustan Unilever Limited (HUL) has taken initiatives to help the poor people especially the women to attain a certain purchasing power and also to earn revenue for the company. Sensing a huge opportunity many automobile companies are trying to woo the rural consumers. Various strategies are being devised and involved to convince the rural consumer for their products. Thus the significance of the rural market has increase due to the saturation, complexity and competitiveness of the urban market and also generating revenue for the economy as a whole.

Indian Scenario

When we consider the scenario of India, there is a picture that comes out; a huge market is created for the developed and manufactured products which make the marketers to move to its hinterlands. There is a large size of rural markets with 742 million people (73 % of the population) and around 200 million households live in the rural areas of India. The Indian rural market has a huge demand base and offers great opportunities to marketers. The union budget for 2009-10 hiked the allocation for the National Rural Employment Guarantee Act (NREGA) to US$ 8.03 billion, giving a further boost to the rural economy. This is in addition to the Farmer waiver loan of US$ 13.86 billion and the ambitious Bharat Nirman Programme with an outlay of US$ 34.84 billion for improving rural infrastructure. Rural markets in India have contributed a fair share of their revenue to the national income of the country.

Area	*Population in 2001*	*Percent*
RuralUrban	742,490,639.286,119,689.	72.227.8

From the table it is clear that two-thirds of the population in India live in the rural areas of the one billion population of India. This size of the population has been witnessing an increase in its income but also in production and consumption. The Indian rural market today accounts for only about Rs 8 billion of the total 120 billion, thus claiming 6.6 percent of the total share. So clearly there seems to be a long road ahead. According to a survey by Mc Kinsey survey, the rural market will be worth US$ 500-600 billion by 2020. Of the 593 rural districts that Mc Kinsey surveyed, 67 were classified as urban cousins, 118 as those close to rural economic centres, around 160 as able districts with a basic minimal infrastructure and 248 districts as deprived. Rural marketing is set to clock 20 percent growth in fiscal 2008-09 with Rs 570 crores of promotional budgets being spent by major companies like AirTel, Hewlett Packard (HP), and Intel etc. on rural marketing and below the line activities. The expansion of India's telecom industry has led to an "all inclusive growth" of the Indian economy in terms of GDP. In 2006-07 the country saw a growth rate of 9.6 percent which is mainly due to the telecom sector. The demand for telecommunication services are surging across rural India, as middle class and upper classes are growing in most villages.

With the next 100 million subscribers coming from the rural areas, many Indian mobile services are targeting the rural consumers with low cost tariffs affordable for the rural consumers. The present trend shows that the Indian rural market is very vast and worth an estimated Rs. 3500 billion out of which Rs.2500 is from the agricultural products. Rural marketing is all set to worth $500-600 billion by 2020 and with the growth of income from the rural sector would set a fast pace for development of the rural areas in India.

Rural Marketing in Meghalaya

Meghalaya with an area of 22,429 sq. km. is one of the smallest states of the Indian Union. It became a separate state in 1972 and before that it was part of Assam. The state has seven districts with 5492 villages. The population of the state is 2.306 million as the 2001 census. Unlike India, where urban and rural areas share the same proportion of poor people, in Meghalaya poverty resides mainly in the rural areas. Except for Shillong which is the capital of Meghalaya and other districts, people living in the rural areas are unexposed to the idea of goods and services being introduced to them. Rural marketing is a new term in Meghalaya which basically is confined to agricultural products. People residing in the rural areas of Meghalaya have a high disposable income, especially those who are involve in services mainly through trade, contracts, government services and those who are involve in non-farm activities or maybe those who own large cultivable land where productivity is sufficient for consumption and selling of their products. Sensing the growth of their per capita disposable income rural consumer is ready to spend on goods and services launched by companies from the nearby urban market. Thus the scenario in Meghalaya changes with company's product being launched in the rural areas which included wide range of products from mobile services, Direct to Home (DTH) services, consumer durables, IT services etc.

Meghalaya has a congenial investment climate with most of the resources confined to the rural areas. 75 percent of the people live in the rural areas. In Meghalaya the socio-economic status is changing in the rural areas and companies are trying to understand the attitude of the people and are ready to invest only in certain particular areas. The reason is because people in the rural areas are unpredictable and they will purchase the goods only if they are loyal brands.

In a survey of sub-districts of Meghalaya like Mawkyrwat and Mairang of West Khasi Hills, Sohra, Mawsynram of East Khasi Hills and Dedengiri in West Garo Hills which are still rural areas, rural marketing has played an important role changing the lives of people through the exploitation of their resources or making them conscious and aware of raising their voices for improvement of their livelihood. The introduction of consumer durables especially television has increases their fascination and the demand for DTH services has increase. This also gave them information related to weather and guidelines for farmers to increase their productivity. Mobile services providers like Aircel, Airtel, Reliance, BSNL has come to these areas with an investment amounting to 2-3 crores in setting up towers, offices, and shops in these areas. It is generating revenue to the companies and at the same time rural consumers, even those who are illiterate are impressed for possessing a mobile and knowing how to use it. People in these areas who are educated are being employed and thus increasing their income level.

Growth of rural marketing is not confined to these sub-districts but Lakhs of promotional budget is spent by these companies in rural marketing in rural areas of Meghalaya like Mawngap, Rongara in Garo hills, Byrnihat in Ri-Bhoi, Nangbah and Ladrymbai in Jaintia Hills, Mawmluh in East Khasi Hills etc.

Even commodities i.e. consumables which are branded are also captivating the rural consumers. People know when they purchase what brand of toothpaste, face creams, food etc. are being sold in the village shops.

The annual durable market like televisions, audio

systems, refrigerators, DTH services, furniture etc. is growing at 7-10%. Even in terms of agricultural inputs it has grown tremendously for those who own large tracts of land for cultivation. It is approximately estimated that Rs 100 crores have spent for agricultural inputs and approximately Rs 200-500 crores for two or four wheelers. In Meghalaya as in the rest of India the rural areas are untapped for automobile services except for Jaintia Hills District in Meghalaya where the per capita disposable income is quite high since it is a coal belt region and where most people are big businessmen.

Thus the concept of rural marketing in Meghalaya is still in an evolving shape as the sector poses various challenges, including understanding the dynamics of rural markets and strategies to supply and understand the rural consumers.

Some of the contributing factors for rural marketing are as follows:

- Better income from agricultural production.
- Spread of education.
- Improved infrastructure.
- Increase penetration of electronic media.
- Life style changes due to education market penetration.
- Most of the income does come from agriculture which is about 50%.
- Increase influence of youth in the buying decisions.

Hurdles in Rural Marketing in Meghalaya

Even though rural marketing has also achieved its significance in rural areas of Meghalaya but there involve a variety of challenges in making it work. The marketing gurus acknowiedge the fact that the urban market especially Shillong has become saturated; hence most of the marketers are being targeted to explore the rural areas in generating revenue. However there are significant challenges to the entire process the most important being the capacity building of the rural entrepreneurs. For decades the entrepreneurs are associated with the traditional knowledge of business, humiliation with government, so they tend to look at these initiatives with skepticism. Only consistent results can convince the rural consumers. In Meghalaya one of the main drawbacks of rural marketing is that it is concentrated in those areas where infrastructure is good or minimal while the vast majority of those living in the rural areas are unexposed to this particular idea. Some of the challenges in Meghalaya regarding rural marketing are highlight as follows:

- There is a high distribution costs because the distribution system is divided into many tiers with middle men wanting to take all the profits.
- There is a huge cultural gap between the urban marketers and the rural consumers.
- In Meghalaya one of the problems is inaccessibility due to poor roads which pose a hindrance in the distribution of the goods to the rural areas.
- There is acute dependence of the people in the vagaries of the monsoons because it is seen that seasonal consumption is linked to harvest and festivals.
- In order to set up a market in the rural areas there is high initial development expenditure especially in those areas where there is electricity shortage-sporadic power supply.

Companies also find it difficult to start a market where there is highly dispersed and thinly populated markets and thus in Meghalaya most of the rural marketing takes place where the population is approximately 5000 to 30000 or above knowing a demand base will be formed with a high population.

Social and cultural backwardness of the masses is one

of the challenges facing a rural consumer. They are being guided by the traditional way of thinking due to their low level of exposure to different product categories and they tend to buy those goods only which they are comfortable or maybe it is a habit for them.

There is a large number of people in the rural areas which are daily wage earners where their income is not being saved but is spent automatically. There is also non-availability of consumer finance options due to various banking and credit problems.

There is also lack of consumer awareness about the various products due to inaccessibility to conventional advertising media.

Key to Success for Rural Marketing

Dynamics of rural markets differ from other markets and also rural marketing strategies should also be different along with the procurement of basic facilities for general development of the rural areas.

The basic facilities needed by the rural areas are the twin objectives of providing health-care and education which can change the perspective of the people for other avenues.

An effective distribution system requires a village level shopkeeper, distributer at the district level and company owned depot, consignment distribution at the state level. This would help in reducing the cost of distribution.

For the development of the rural market the 4 A's work

- Availability of the product
- Affordability because the rural consumer is sensitive to price and thus one of the strategies taken by GODREJ is to introduce the products in small packs e.g. Cinthol and Fairglow at 50 gm are priced at Rs. 4.
- Acceptability by offering products to suit the rural markets e.g. DTH services are provided at lower costs in rural areas.

Awareness by using different means of advertisement. Companies can launched their products in the haats, weekly or bi-weekly markets taking place. By putting up posters, billboards, radios etc.

Rural market faces the critical issues of distribution, understanding the rural consumer, communication and poor infrastructure. The marketer has to strengthen the distribution and price strategies. The rural consumer expects value for money since he has an unsteady and meager income, increasing the household income and improving distribution are the viable strategies that have to be adapted to tap the immense potential.

Nowadays educated rural youth can also influence the rural consumers because they are influenced by the life style they watch in television sets. The penetration of media exposes them in their buying behavior immensely.

Conclusion

Empowering the rural areas means developing the capacity so that they can be confident to act on their own choices. Rural marketing helps in creating a market for them to enhance their skills making them more confident. Rural marketing is an evolving concept, and as a part of any economy has untapped potential; marketers have realized only recently. The rural population has shown a trend of change and it is also changing them to move to a state of gradual urbanization in terms of exposure, habits, lifestyles and lastly consumption patterns of goods and services. The rural market is not a separate entity and is highly influenced by the sociological and behavioral factors operating in the country. Rural marketing can be viewed as a way of exploiting income of the rural consumers but it is innovative if people know how to use it due to the creation of a market by these companies and the information delivered by them. Thus it helps in reducing knowledge gaps and sharing information on economic values for farmers and others which is an essential input for increasing productivity and boosting growth in the rural areas. The rural consumer is looking at better options for higher returns on their surplus earnings.

However in rural India or Meghalaya lacks a good distribution system since they exhibit an "earn today, spend today" mentality because they tend to buy only those goods which are of immediate requirements no matter what their income level might be.

To succeed, companies and entrepreneurs need to understand the mindset and psyche of the people which may be difficult along with a good distribution network.

REFERENCES

A Development Approach from *Vikalpa* (July-September 1985),A journal in English, published by IIMA

http:/www.rural relations.com/ppt/Group%2011.ppt.

K.L.K.Rao and Ramesh Tagat, *Rural Marketing-a development approach*

N.Rajendhiran, *Rural Marketing – A Critical approach*

Sukhpal Singh, *Rural Marketing Management*

T. Sivagnana Selvakumar, *Rural Marketing; Facts For You*, April 2009

5

Is the Lack of Governance Impeding the Development Process in Meghalaya?

Dhiraj K. Borkotoky

It has been nearly forty years since Meghalaya achieved its statehood. The leaders who had fought for the Hill State Movement had a vision of governing and guiding their own future. But nearly forty years down the line the vision of a better future has to a larger extent remained dormant. Meghalaya also known as the 'abode of clouds' with all its potential resources – both renewable and non-renewable— has been lagging behind many other states due to various reasons. Meghalaya has always been an agricultural state with a majority of its population being dependent on agriculture for its livelihood. An overwhelming majority of its population in the state is rural based (more than 80%), and hence the focus on the rural issues should have been a major thrust area of the state. It can be safely stated that the state lacks a proper vision for the development of the rural areas.

One has to understand that there is a serious problem which is impeding the process of development in the state and the most important factor that is affecting the process of development is that of lack of 'EFFECTIVE GOVERNANCE' in the state of Meghalaya. There is a general tendency among the masses to use a phrase "there is no governance in this state and this has led to the failure of development in the state". Hence it becomes very important for us to understand what 'GOVERNANCE 'is exactly, and its relation to the process of development in the state of Meghalaya.

It is fair to say that until the late 1980's, governance was not a word heard frequently within the development community. But today it is a buzzword used freely in most publications emanating from the government departments, donor agencies and academics. Governance was first problematised in a World Bank document of 1989 on Sub-Saharan Africa which suggested that the lack of development was related to a crisis in governance. The Bank defines governance as "...the exercise of political power to manage a nation's economic and social resources for development". It meant the institutional capacity of public organizations to provide the public and other goods demanded by a country's citizens in an effective, transparent, impartial and accountable manner. For governance to be visible there has to be four distinct features: (1) a responsible and responsive administrative-bureaucratic management, (2) a clear and visionary framework for development, (3) transparency and accountability, and (4) informed and conscious civil society. Thus the World Bank's definition is linked to participatory development, human rights and democratization. This conception of governance enjoins legitimacy of government; accountability of political elements of government; competence of governments to make policies and deliver services; and respect for human rights and the rule of law. At the same time it is not difficult to figure out what is bad governance. The World Bank itself finds certain features to tell what is bad governance:- these are (1) failure to make clear separation between what is public and what is private which leads to a diversion of public resources for private purpose/ gains, (2) failure to establish a predictable framework of due process of law leading to authoritarian rule and oligarchy; (3) red tapism , excessive rules and regulations , cumbersome and corrupt licensing requirement, slow movement of official procedure; and (4) misallocation of resources and inconsistent priorities.

One of the most simple and lucid perspective given on governance is by Stoker who lays down five dimensions of governance:

(a) Governance refers to a complex set of institutions and actors that are drawn from but also beyond the government.

(b) Governance recognizes the blurring of boundaries and responsibilities for tackling social and economic issues.

(c) Governance identifies the power dependence involved in the relationship between institutions involved in collective action.

(d) Governance is about autonomous self-governing networks of actors.

(e) Governance recognizes the capacity to get things done which does not rest on the power of the government to command or use its authority. It sees government as able top use new tools and techniques to steer and guide.

Governance in Meghalaya

Each country has its own history and context and hence there is no universal model of good governance. India is a developing country and the importance of good governance for its development can in no cost be relegated to the background, but we have to remember that in India the concept of governance has been mainly seen as something that can eradicate poverty, implementing the policies of the government etc, removing corruption and increasing the idea of accountability and transparency. It is the state in India which holds the most important place in the entire process of development. But in the state of Meghalaya the situation has been very much intriguing as the concept of governance gets evaporated in the fight among the institutions of governance in the state. We can look into the three important levels of institutions, viz., the state government, the Autonomous District Councils and the traditional local self-governing institutions. There is governance when the functioning of institutions in a web of relationship leads to development. But in Meghalaya this is not happening because there is too much of overlapping of powers, internal bickering among the various institutions of governance—the end result is that the entire concept of development takes a beating and the common masses have to suffer for no fault of theirs. The people of Meghalaya especially the rural poor have been bereft of governance in view of the institutional crisis which can be send in the manner in which the state government and the District Councils function. The institutions of democracy are at loggerheads with each other and this is not a good sign for proper governance. The Vision 2020 Document prepared by the North Eastern Council puts a greater emphasis on good governance, including governance at the grassroots level through the institutions of self government, but this is not happening in the state of Meghalaya.

Governance requires that mechanisms, process and institutions that will acquire and subsequently apply public resources to fulfill priority areas of 'public good'. In Meghalaya the institutions of governance are no doubt there but how they respond to the public god is extremely doubtful. It is well accepted that the political regime and its stability is one of the major ingredients to usher in good governance. But in the small state of Meghalaya, political instability is one of the major factors why governance is ineffective today — we already had more that twenty different governments for a period of around forty years. Putting it in simple terms, it means on an average there has been a change of political regime after every two years. This political instability does not augur well for the all - round development of the state. The Development Economists have emphasized on the fact that political stability is one of the most important aspects of healthy governance, but our state lacks such dynamic leaders with vision who could emphasize on political stability. In the state of Meghalaya the short term gains are more important then the long term gains for a section of the society and this affects the common masses in a harmful manner.

The important question is how lack of effective governance can have a negative impact on the scenario of rural development in Meghalaya. The Central schemes of improving the rural livelihood are abound such as NREGS, BRGF, IAY, SGSY, IWDP, but the question is how far such schemes have been successful in improving the living standards of the rural masses. To have a broader understanding of the successes of such schemes, we have to understand which are the institutions involved in implementing such programmes. Many rural development schemes are actually implemented by the state government itself through the Block Offices. At present there are two committees known as the Block Development Committee (B.D.C) and the Block Selection Committee (B.S.C). These two committees are the ones that select the beneficiaries of the various schemes. But is seems that the members of these two committees are selected government in power without consultation. Secondly, these committees have not been brought under the purview of any law. These committees are not accountable to the people and are given freedom to exercise their authority without any control. Thus it means that it is the insti6tution of the state government alone which is involved with the process of rural development. But good governance also means that there has to be recognition of spatial distribution of power and its multiple centres. These centres can be at various spatial levels rising from the local community itself. Thus participation and de-centralisation are key elements in the current discourse on democratic governance. In an era where de-centralisation is the buzzword, Meghalaya focuses more on centralisation, but it is not possible that the modern welfare state can look into all aspect of people's life and hence there is a greater need for de-centralisation, but this is not to be in this state, in fact there is a tendency for more centralisation. In other states of the country, the institutions of local self governments, i.e, the Panchayati Raj Institutions plays a vital role in the process of implementation of rural schemes such as the National Rural Employment Guarantee Scheme. But the state of Meghalaya had been kept out of the purview of the 73rd Constitutional Amendment which rationalized the entire concept of local self governance. In lieu of such institutions it was expected that institutions such as the local self governing institutions and the ADCs would have had a greater say in the process of development. But these institutions were deliberately kept out of the process of development. The ADCs have become very much redundant with no development priorities and this has led to its malfunction in various areas, the state government also keeps the ADCs under strict control by using Para 12 A of the Sixth Schedule. On the other hand the traditional institutions of the tribal people are also ignored not only by the state government but also by the ADCs. In fact these institutions should have been entrusted with some amount of responsibility towards the process of development.

Robert Putnam talks about the concept of 'SOCIAL CAPITAL' as an important agent in the process of development. The vast amount of social capital that is traditionally available in the tribal societies such as that of the Durbar Shnong has been never made use of in the rural development process. The prevalence of a strong and responsible civil society is very important for the process of good governance. This means that governance does not only come from the administrative-government structure, but also from the civil society which cannot shrink away from its responsibility of acting as a social and development agents. The idea of 'Social Audit' in matters of Centrally as well as state sponsored schemes is virtually non existent, and it is the civil society which can play a very important role in the process of social audit which can keep the state government under a tight check. It is important that the traditional institutions should adjust in time to the fast pace of change and start playing an important role in the process of rural upliftment.

For a fast and rapid upliftment of the rural sector it is very important to follow Stoker's two important dimensions, namely, governance recognizes the blurring of boundaries and responsibilities for tackling of social and economic issues and that governance identifies the power dependence involved in the relationship between institutions involved in collective action. These two dimensions are very important for the process of development in the hill state of Meghalaya. In this respect it is very important that the institutions of governance comes together and contribute towards the process of development instead of looking for opportunities to cut one another's throat. The institutions which can help uplift the process of rural development are already there, but it is a question of how they come together keeping aside their differences for the process of development. It is high time that the vast amount of social capital that is available be made use to augment the development process of Meghalaya.

REFERENCES

1) Study on Functioning, Structure of Local Governance in North Eastern Region with special reference to Autonomous District Councils': A Report submitted to the Commission on Centre-state Relations by NEHU 2009.

2) 'Good Governance for Transformation and Development of Meghalaya', by ICARE, C/O Toki Blah, 2007.

3) Niraja Jayal Gopal, The Governance Agenda: Making Democratic Development Dispensable in *Economic and Political Weekly*, February 1997.

4) Adrian Leftwich, Governance, democracy and development in the Third World in *The Third World Quarterly*, 1993.

5) C.J.Thomas, *Engagement and Development: India's North East and Neighboring countries.*

6) Dr. L.S. Gassah, A Report on The Autonomous District Council in the Khasi Hills: A Critical Analysis.

7) Kuldeep Mathur, From Government to Governance.

8) The North Eastern Region Vision 2020, the Ministry of Development of North Eastern Region.

6

Re-Evaluating the Potential of Bamboo Shoot for Enhancement of Rural Livelihood: A Case Study of Ribhoi District, Meghalaya

K.Nongrum, D.D.Nengnong, K. Rabha & A.P. Warjri

Introduction

The existence of man on the surface of the earth has been based directly or indirectly on his ability to exploit the natural resources (biotic and abiotic) that are found in the natural surroundings. Initially the earth was adequately blessed with geo-environmental resources that have evolved through time to sustain the carrying capacity for all types of environments or ecosystem found on its surface. Some ecosystems are very rich in life forms while others are rather poor, depending on the geographical factors and their ability to adapt to the varied environmental conditions. Hence the distribution of all natural resources (especially the living) is not evenly distributed throughout the globe and certainly not in our country as well. The pressure of population growth, urbanization, and the advent of modern agricultural practices and the ever changing nature of the natural landscape to the cultural one due to human encroachment and interferences has affected the stability of the ecosystem as a whole. Furthermore, the quest for higher economic development, better standard of living, the increasing nature of consumerism, coupled with the uses of powerful and effective technologies in extracting the natural resources have resulted in the rapid depletion of all these resources and many of them are lost forever or on the verge of extinct.

Today, even with all the best efforts to enhance the quality of life through his hard work and ingenuity, man still fall short of his expectations and continue to face a life full of hardship and uncertainty. Much of the means to earn his livelihood (be it traditional or modern techniques), have not been able to deliver him perfect result and desirable satisfaction, instead most of his efforts are plagued with failure and wasteful utilization of all natural resources. Many a times his activities prove to be detrimental for the whole system, (especially the living counterpart). He himself too often becomes a part of the tragedy when complex problems set in, compounding one on top of the other without any solution in sight. No matter how much nations boast the success of their economy, none can deny the short comings and failures their society's experiences in many fronts in their day to day life (especially in developing nations like our own). More than 75% of India's population lives in the rural areas. Their daily life revolves around primary activities such as agriculture and extracting resources from the natural environment for which the forests provides much of their requirements. With about 40% of the country's population living below or hovering around poverty line and struggling for survival on meager resources and employment opportunity, it is about time that the country needs to rethink and overhaul its strategy in order to mitigate and overcome this crisis by re-evaluating our forest resources and to come up with more down to earth ,realistic, effective, profit maximizing, minimum wastage, eco-friendly and sustainable devices in the utilization of our forest resources for the development and security of the rural populace at large.

Locating entirely in the northern tropical region (8 4' to 37 6' north latitude and 68 07' to 97 25' east longitude) the country covers an area of about 3.28 million square kilometers. With its diverse topographical features of extensive mountain ranges, plains, plateaus, coastal regions and islands, the country also experiences a wide range of climatic variation. Extreme climatic condition is common in the sub-continent, either it is too hot like in Jaisalmer where the mercury can touch 45 C or more or very cold like in Leh where it can dip to as low as -30 C. On the other hand it can be as wet with 1300cms of rainfall at Mawsynram or as dry with less than 25cms in the desert region of Rajasthan. It is also not strange that the country can experience both floods and drought almost at the same time. However on the whole, the country enjoys a favorable monsoonal type of climate throughout and very conducive for supporting a very rich biodiversity.

India is identified as one of the 12 mega-diversity centre of the world. The north eastern states together comprises as one of the richest biodiversity region amongst the many found in the country. All types of biodiversity are found in this region such as genetic, specific, ecological, domesticated and microbial. However with the rapid depletion of living forms due to human activities and interferences, together with the other biodiversity reserves of the country, i.e. the Eastern Himalayas, the Western Ghats, and the Andaman and Nicobar islands, it has now become a biodiversity hotspot that is of global concern. This rich bio-diversity is spread throughout the country and have evolved and survived here for hundreds of years. Many of them are endemic to this country. In brief, on the whole the country possesses about 49000 species of plants which account to more than 7% of the world flora. 15,000 are flowering plants out of which about 5000 are endemic to the country itself (MOEF, 1994).On the other hand, the country is also equally rich in term of its fauna. It has more than 70,000 animal species which account to about 6.4% of the world. It is amazing to note that within an area of about 3.28 million sq km that account to only 2.4% of the total land area of the world, to sustain 5% of the flora and fauna of the world. The nation stands at 10th position in terms of bio-diversity richness.

Like the rest of the other bio-sphere reserves of the country, Meghalaya, situating within the north eastern region is also very rich in bio-diversity. In fact it boasts the presence of important bio-sphere reserve at Nokrek, the Balpakram National Park and many more within its territory. The whole landscape itself is inhabited and supporting a variety of life forms, some of which are unique to the state itself. Without a doubt, comparing with the Khasi and Jaintia Hills perhaps Ribhoi district with its favorable physical conditions harbors the maximum number of flora and fauna species. The presence of the Nongkhyllem Wildlife Sanctuary, the Kharsati Park and the many sacred groves will confirm this statement.

BASIC FACTS OF RIBHOI DISTRICT

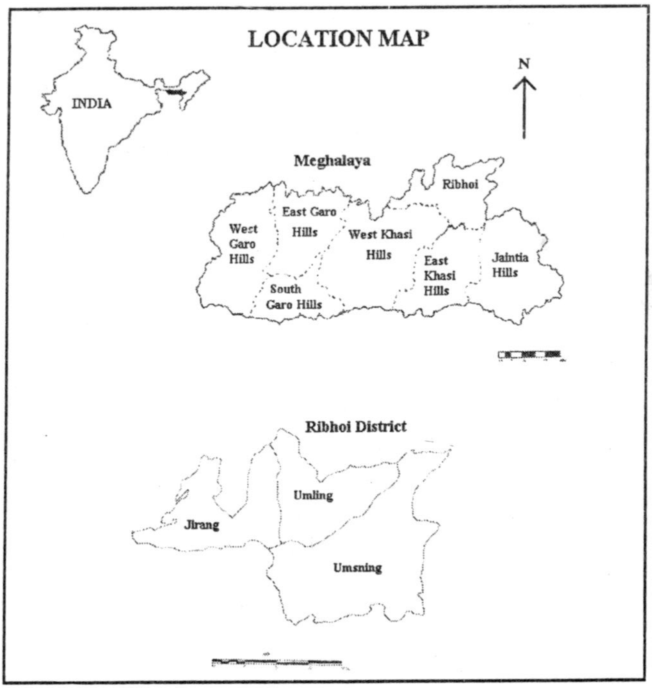

Headquarter	:	Nongpoh.
Location Latitude	:	25° 35' to 26° 10' North
Longitude.		91° 12' to 92° 12' East
Area	:	2448 Sq.Kms.
C & RD Blocks	:	Three (3)
	1.	Umling (857.3 Sq.Kms)
	2.	Umsning (1105 Sq.Kms)
	3.	Jirang (485.7 Sq.Kms)
Population	:	192790
Literacy rate	:	65.7%
Physiography	:	Low senile topography (65 mts – 1000 mts) Slope – 25° Average.
Drainage	:	Umtrew, Umiam, Umran.
Soil	:	Laterite and alluvial.
Climate	:	Monsoon type.
Fauna	:	Nonkhyllem, Kharsati wild life sanctuary.
Vegetation	:	Mixed tropical forest (rich in biodiversity)
Ethnic group	:	Khasi (Bhoi), Garos, Marngar, Rabha, Mikirs, and non tribals.
Culture	:	Rich.
Religious group	:	Multi and tribal.
Urbanization	:	low (6%)
Occupational structure	:	Basically traditional/ subsistence

		Agrarian- 80% shifting/ sedentary/others
		Formal sector – 6% trade and commerce
		Transport etc – 14%.
Agricultural Products	:	Mainly rice, maize, ginger, banana etc.
Animal Husbandry	:	Bee keeping, poultry, piggery etc.

The term Ri-Bhoi or the country of the mountain people has always been synonym with a landscape covered in thick jungle and a haven for wild life and inhabited by simple tribal folks, who even though poor, have lived a contended and secured life in perfect harmony with the environment for ages. With the attainment of statehood on the 21th January 1972, and with a quest for rapid economic development, the region is now able to boast of the progress it has made in numerous avenues, however on the other hand the losses of its natural environment especially the diverse living organisms has outweigh all the gains. Close studies on the society of the Ribhoi district, (especially the condition of weaker section) reveal a situation which is not at all appealing. It reflects the discontentment and insecurity amongst the people and it is also feared that if this trend continues, many will stand to lose everything while the gains would be harvested by only a few.

At present, like the other rural areas of the state and the region as a whole, the people of Ri-Bhoi district would have to turn back to the forest for sustenance and to salvage whatever it is left to revive their socio-economic and cultural identity. However, in view of the problem of the environmental degradation, at present the only surviving forest product that have the potential to sustain and revive the rural economy of Ribhoi district that is still available in the forest, would unmistakably be the poor man's timber itself which is the' bamboo'. Keeping in mind the multi-functional potential that bamboo possesses and its tested services to mankind all over the world since ancient times, the present paper entitled "*Re-evaluating the potential of bamboo shoot for enhancement of rural livelihood* ", (A case study of Ribhoi District of Meghalaya), is an attempt to study and further reveal specifically, the potential of bamboo shoot as a commercial food item. It is believe that if aided by the application of simple innovative technology which is manageable by the village folks themselves to enhance the overall market value of all products made from bamboo shoot, without a doubt, coupled with awareness, positive attitude and sincere effort from the people themselves, the full potential of this wonder plant which has been rightly dubbed as 'Green Gold' will surely help in supplementing and uplifting the rural livelihood of Ribhoi district as a whole.

Bamboo

Bamboos belong to the true grass family Poaceae (or Gramineae) subfamily Bambusoideae, tribe Bambuseae. There are more than 70 genera of bamboos divided into about 1000 species. Bamboos are fast growing tall tree like grasses with woody hollow aerial stems that branch out in clusters from a thick rhizome. Their growth rate can be as high as 60 centimeters (24 inches) per day but is highly dependent on the local soil and climatic conditions and the unique rhizome-depending system. Bamboos often form dense undergrowth that excludes other plants. Bamboo possesses an in exhaustive utility and has provided man with all his needs from simple ones such as food, clothing and shelter to all our higher needs which include employment, education, health, and the list goes on and on. Bamboos are found in tropical and sub-tropical to mild temperate regions of the world (from 50 north latitude to 47 south latitude) and are also found surviving up to altitude of about 3500 meters above mean sea level. In India, bamboos abundantly occurs in the tropical moist and dry forest of North East India, Andhra Pradesh, Orissa, Maharashtra, Karnataka, Tami Nadu and Bihar. India has about 18 genera and 136 species of bamboos for which more than 50% is found in the North Eastern Region. According to the Planning Commission (1965) bamboo occupy 1, 00209 sq km of the country's forest area and generated more than 4000 million tones of bamboos per year. Out of the total annual production of bamboos in the country, about 32% is use in construction work, 30% in rural uses, 17% for pulp making, 7% for packing and the remaining 14% for other uses. Second only to China, yet the country has not been able to tap this resource effectively (only about 15%) even with a favorable international market in bamboo worth more than 14 billion US dollar annually.

Table1: Production of Bamboos in India

Sl. No.	*States/U.Territorries*	*Area in sq km*	*Production in thousand tonnes*
1	Andhra Pradesh	19,700	255
2	Assam	10,000	1210
3	Bihar	5254	200
4	Gujarat	1936	46
5	Himachal Pradesh	104	3
6	Karnataka	6000	475
7	Kerela	631	108
8	Madhya Pradesh	14364	800
9	Maharashtra	8500	300
10	Manipur	2500	-
11	Orissa	10500	439
12	Punjab	-	9
13	Tamil Nadu	5388	-
14	Tripura	2849	215
15	Uttar Pradesh	4000	41
16	West Bengal	164	8
17	Arunachal Pradesh	7779	200
	India	**100200**	**4309**

Sources: Planning Commission Report.

Table2: Uses of bamboo in India

Uses	*In (%)*
Construction work	32%
Rural uses	30%
Pulp/paper industry	17%
Packing	07%
Other uses	14%
Total	100%

Source: Planning Commission Report.

Note: Only 15% -20%of bamboo is utilized in India annually.

Bamboo in Meghalaya

With favorable geographical conditions, the extent of natural bamboo forests in Meghalaya has been estimated to be 3108 sq kilometers (FSI Inventory Report, 1990), which is about 14 % of the total geographical area of the state. It has been estimated that the bamboo forest in the state bears 471 million equivalents of sound culms of bamboo. The weight of this Bamboo stock has been estimated to be 2.6 million tonnes, and considering felling cycle of 4 years, the potential yield of bamboo in the state is still a good 2.09 tonnes /ha/ year.. Scanning some 20 topographical maps of the region it is noticed that bamboo grooves form an important part and parcel of the forest cover of the state, right from the flood plains of Garo hills to the high ridges of the Shillong plateau. However their occurrences decrease with increasing altitude and they are more abundant below 1000 meters contour. The low rolling topography of Ribhoi district is a landscape known for its rich biodiversity, also has a fair share of many species of this plant (about 40 of them). More than 45 species of bamboos are found in the state (Khongsit, 1999), but some species such as *Dendrocalamus hamiltonii, Dendrocalamus giganteaus, Bambusa bamboo, Cephalostychum latifolium, Meloncana bamboosoides*, etc are very common in Meghalaya.

Large part of the bamboo comes from the abandoned 'jhum' areas of Ribhoi district where it grows in gregarious manner as a colonizer. People harvest bamboo from the areas belonging to their respective communities. Bamboos possess utility that surpasses even our wildest expectation and have provided basic needs such as food, shelter, tools for man including supporting his development in thick and thin for thousands of years till date.

Bamboo Shoot Production at Ribhoi District

Keeping in mind the multi-functionality of bamboo which is indeed very vast, like in the rest of the world where ever bamboo plant is found, bamboo shoots are part and

Table 3: Bamboo species of Meghalaya

Sl. No.	*Species*
1	*Arundinaria hirsute*
2	*Arundinaria mannii*
3	*Arundinaria microphylla*
4	*Arundinaria suberecta*
5	*Bambusa arundinacea*
6	*Bambusa balcooa*
7	*Bambusa glauscescens* = Bambusa nana*
8	*Bambusa khasiana*
9	*Bambusa longispiculata*
10	*Bambusa nutans*
11	*Bambusa pallida*
12	*Bambusa tulda*
13	*Bambusa vulgaris**
14	*Cephalostachyum capitatum*
15	*Var. decompositum*
16	*Cephalostachyum fuchsianum*
17	*Cephalostachyum pallidum*
18	*Cephalostachyum griffithiana = Arundinaria griffithiana*
19	*Cephalostachyum hookeriana = Arundinaria polystachys*
20	*Cephalostachyum khasiana = Arundinaria khasiana*
21	*Cephalostachyum polystachya = Arundinaria polystachya*
22	*Dendrocalamus calostachys*
23	*Dendrocalamus hamiltonii*
24	*Dendrocalamus hookeri*
25	*Dendrocalamus sikkimensis*
26	*Dendrocalamus strictus*
27	*Dinochloa compactiflora = Melocalamus compacitiflorus*
28	*Gigantochloa macrostachya*
29	*Gigantochloa takeserah*

30	*Melocanna baccifera = Melocanna bambusoides*
31	*Neohouzeoua dullooa*
32	*Neohouzeoua helferi*
33	*Oxytenanthera albociliata**
34	*Oxytenanthera nigrociliata*
35	*Phyllostachys mannii*
36	*Pseudostachyum polymorphum*
37	*Teinostachyum griffithii*
38	*Thamnocalamus prainii = Arundinaria prainii*

Source: Department of Forest and Environment of Meghalaya.

Table 4: Areas under bamboo cultivation in Meghalaya

Region	*Clump Forming*		*Non-clump Forming*	
	Area (in sq km)	*Growing Stock (in tones)*	*Area (in sq km)*	*Growing Stock (in tones)*
Khasi Hills	1658.20	1286229.4	71.32	91174.3
Jaintia Hills	140.18	108734.6	0	0.0
Garo Hills	831.80	645209.0	329.9	512912.7
Total	2630.18	2040173.0	401.22	604087.0

Forest Survey of India's Report 1987.

parcel of the natural diet of the people of Ribhoi district as a whole. It is naturally available during the monsoon season, highly nutritious and a versatile food stuff that can be prepared and consumed fresh, as pickles or as fermented in numerous ways and also be stored for future use. It is also a well sorted seasonal delicacy for city dwellers who pays generously for these simple forest products.

Harvesting Shoots - A good clump structure for plantations devoted to shoot production is in the ratio of 4:4:2, for the first, second and third years, respectively. In timber-cum-shoot plantations, as a thumb rule for plantations devoted to only shoot production, 50-60 percent of the shoots can be harvested every year.

Table 5: Extractability of different species of bamboo

No.	*Name of the Species*	*Edible portion*
1	*Dendrocalamus hamiltonii*	45.75%
2	*Dendrocalamus longispathus*	40.00%
3	*Dendrocalamus brandisii*	32.61%
4	*Dendrocalamus strictus*	20.80%
5	*Bambusa bambos*	30.25%
6	*Bambusa tulda*	19.84%

Table 6: Given below is the bamboo shoot production/year recorded at Chessa, Arunachal Pradesh (Data collected by the State Forest Research Institute, Itanagar)

Bamboo spp	*Average annual number of shoots per clump*	*Period of shoot emergence*
Bambusa balcooa	25	June-July
Bambusa nutans	13	March-September
Bambusa pallida	41	July
Bambusa polymorpha	34	June-July
Bambusa tulda	17	May-July
Dendrocalamus giganteus	7	June-July
Dendrocalamus hamiltonii	52	July-September
Gigntochloa macrostachya	13	July
Melocanna bambusoides	90	July-August
Phyllostachys bambusoides	53	March-May

The shoot production and timing differs from one species to another and each species can produce shoots for about 6 months, but the peak will be very short. It is also worthwhile to note that the extractability amongst species is different. Perhaps the most common species found in Ribhoi district, (*Dendrocalamus hamiltonii*) is the most productive of all with 45.75% of edible portion and high yielding of about 52 shoots per clump. With the shoot season of different species peaking at different time, maximum shoots can be extracted for a longer period. Till date bamboo shoot is not a significant forest product worth considering when compared to mature bamboo which have a wide range of utility thus commercially very valuable. In the rural areas of Ribhoi district it is simply a seasonal food source mainly for home consumption and only a small surplus is put out for sale, that to, only in those areas connected by roads. Even in the local weekly markets bamboo shoot products is not that important.

Study revealed that till date the production of this resource is uncertain as it is seasonal and the method of harvesting is not regular and systematic. However for the last two years of study in the region, it is roughly estimated that about 8 to 10 tonnes of bamboo shoots are collected fresh from the forest per season (maximum 3-4 months). Out of this, hardly one- third enters the market. Coupled with ignorance and lack of professionalism these simple folks could make only a meager income with an average of about Rs 2000 to Rs 2500 per season. At present about 1500 individuals are directly involve in the collection of bamboo shoots from groves and jungles and less than 1000 are engaged in marketing this product in the whole district. As it is a seasonal activity, it is mostly taken as a casual part time job. Therefore on an average, after considering all the odds, it is estimated the bamboo shoot trade in the district can just be around Rs 25 lakhs per season.

Table 7: Production of bamboo shoot and monetary value per season, Ribhoi District

Number of individuals engage in collecting bamboo shoots	1500 approximately, mostly casual/part time
Approximate amount collected per season (3-4 months)	8 to 10 tonnes
Average turnover per season for each collector	Rs 2000 to Rs 2500
Number of persons engage in the sale of bamboo shoot products(i.e. the traders)	Rs1000 approximately
Estimate trade on bamboo shoot products per season	Rs 20 to Rs 25 lakhs

Source: Field survey 2007-2009

Table 8: Bamboo species of Ribhoi District used for harvesting shoots

Sl no	*Species*	*Status*	*Usage %*	*Mode of use*	*Food grade (by users)*
1	*Dendrocalamus hamiltonii*	Wild, Abundant	97.00	Fresh, Preserved	Very good
2	*Bambusa balcooa*	Cultivated, Common	0.50	Fresh, Preserved	Excellent, but more culms value
3	*Melocanna bam busoides*	Wild, Common	1.00	Fresh, Preserved	Good
4	*Bambusa polymorpha*	Cultivated, Common	1.25	Fresh, Preserved	Very good
5	*Bambusa tulda*	Cultivated, Common	0.25	Fresh	Good, less preferred

Source: Field survey 2007-2009

Prospect in Bamboo Shoot Trade

With lack of employment opportunities in the district as a whole, it is high time that the people of Ri-Bhoi District should seriously venture into other employment avenues to enhance their livelihood and security. Yet considering their simplicity, their lack of awareness, unexposed, and poverty, it is easier said than done. Due to these weaknesses, it is advisable and more appropriate for them at this juncture to develop their skill and knowledge in those types of activities which they are acquainted rather than risking into other fields that are alien to them. It is observed that with all types of developmental activities creeping into the region, and with better accessibility some people have taken this as an opportunity and have started cashing in on other forest products such as orchids, mushroom, medicinal plants etc. Bamboo shoot trade has appeared as another means of earning their livelihood. However the effort is still in the incipient stage. It is however, very rudimentary, traditional and limited. The sale of this item is in a simple form, usually raw, fermented or pickled according to their suitability, and is sold in weekly markets across the district and on roadsides. Moreover bamboo shoots are seasonal commodities, hence most people have not yet realized or trust on the potential and the ability it has in enhancing their livelihood.

Bamboo shoot is a traditional product of the north eastern region. Except for some hilly tracts in the northern and southern India, it is relatively unknown and not a traditional product in the rest of the country. Therefore the scope of its market, at present is limited only in this region. Yet in this present age of globalization, when things and situations, can change so suddenly, no one can tell about the prospect of any commodity, even for the humble bamboo shoot. Looking beyond our border towards the east, the prospect for bamboo shoot product looks more positive. In fact because of the similar food habit and the huge population present in the South East Asia and East Asia including China, the demand for bamboo shoot products surely is a very huge one. This is very encouraging indeed, and it is about time the people of Ri-Bhoi District are aware of this development. The current effort of the Indian Government to strengthen relationship with nations in the east including China (especially in trade and commerce) through the Look East Policy should also be seriously take note of. In this highly competitive age, only awareness of the changes around us will not be sufficient.

Table 9: Market products of bamboo shoots sold by villagers in Ribhoi District, Meghalaya

Sl no	*Types*	*Market share (%)*	*Market type*	*Market status*	*Consumer preference*
1	Fresh (whole: cleaned/unclean)	26	Local	Seasonal (July-September)	High
2	Fresh chipped	17.8	Local	Seasonal (July-September)	Good
3	Fermented(wet)	14	Regional	July-January	Good
4.	Fermented(dry)	1.2	Local	December-January	Moderate
5	Fermented in running water	0.8	Local	December-January	Good
6	Fermented in soaked mud (Ktieh)	0.2	Local	December-January	High demand
7	Fermented in Suspended bamboo baskets	0.5	Local	December-January	High demand
8	Pickledin mustard oil and salt	8.3	Regional	Perennial	Good
9	Pickledin mustard oil withlocal chilly and salt	13.2	Regional	Perennial	Good
10.	Pickledin mustard oil with chilly, ginger and salt	10.00	Regional	Perennial	Good
11.	Pickledin mustard oil with chilly and salt and ground spices	6.00	Regional	Perennial	Good

Source: Field Survey 2007-2009

These developments can act as a spring board that could bring positive change into the region. There is hope that if the people of this region are ready and able to grab these types of opportunities when it come their way. Therefore the people of Ri-Bhoi District at this juncture should gear up and come out with effective application, innovation and utilization of technology, and resources including the enhancement of human efficiency that will ensure higher production and better quality products of bamboo shoots both for the home and international markets. Only with this attitude, innovative uses of resources such as bamboo shoots or any other will be thoroughly and economically utilize with least wastage thus the livelihood of the people in the region will be enhance and progress in a desirable direction will be in sight.

Means for Enhancing the Market Value of Bamboo Shoot Products

The reason that have retarded the economic development of Ri-Bhoi district for so long is partly due to the usual governmental lacunae in the implementation of various developmental schemes in the region and also the simplicity, ignorance and lack of professionalism amongst the people themselves in going about in their daily livelihood . Thus, in order to bring about a positive change in their economic life, especially in the production and marketing of all the products they produce or extract from their environment, (in this case the production and marketing of bamboo shoot products), it is advisable that the people should come forward and form amongst themselves professional and accountable business organizations with recognize brand name to administer and regulate the production and marketing of traditional bamboo shoot products or any other. All these organizations should be registered and subjected to Government rules and regulations. Bamboo shoot businesses should be examined for the possibility of its development and growth however should adhere to Forest laws and policies to prevent over exploitation of the resource. Local entrepreneurs should be encourage to set up low cost simple machine run units to process and produce bamboo shoot products under recognizable brands subjected to specified government norms. NGOs and other organizations such as the Rural Resource Training Centre (RRTC) Umsning, Self Help Groups (SHG), Government departments, colleges, universities, industrial developing agencies to name a few, should come forward in imparting knowledge, training and enhancing skills and techniques to the villagers in the management and the handling of machines and tools related to the overall processing and production of bamboo shoot items. Government initiatives, policies, including banking and insurance facilities should be provided to promote bamboo shoot production in the district. These business organizations should be able to come up with feasible modification and standardization of the traditional methods of Bamboo Shoot marketing in line with standard food stuff processing, production, packaging under specific authentic brand name as per rule and regulation. All branded bamboo shoot products should be subjected to consumer forum rules and regulation to promote faith and trust amongst the producers and the consumers including accountability. The government as well as the NGOs and other organizations should encourage local people in innovative utilization of raw materials from the forest with simple technology (e.g. using of bamboo cylinders for packing of bamboo shoot items, etc to add more value to the product); this will minimize wastage and also increase employment opportunity for them. The culinary potentials and, nutritional qualities of bamboo shoot are to be ascertained and evaluated scientifically and exhibit in all products. The producers are to see that only permitted standard preservatives and other ingredients used in bamboo shoot products should be as per norm. It would be appealing to see that bamboo shoot products are marketed in a standardized manner where the content/grade/labeling/packaging/pricing/ manufacturing and expiry date are carefully designed and displayed professionally as per rule and regulation. Last but not least, concern authorities should make sure that transport and storage facilities are reliable and adequate to ensure smooth and consistent flow of all products including bamboo shoot.

Marketing and Advertisement

Another important factor that these business organizations, dealing in bamboo shoot products needed to be aware of is that the popularizing and marketing of any product needs good and effective advertisement. Therefore to expose Bamboo shoot product to a wider national and international market, the need for a reliable and sustaining exchange of information, experiences and marketing expertise is vital. This will bring about an understanding of the marketing network and how global market really operates. Through these types of interactions, our producers will be informed about the demand of the product at various markets whereby they will be able to set up bases and link-up for the supply of the product. Efforts also should be made in showcasing these products using catchy advertisement through media (print and electronic) etc. Events such as fairs/trade expo, seasonal food craft and festivals at all levels (local, national and international) should be encourage and held regularly to promote the marketing of these products.

Conclusion

To conclude, keeping in mind the need to preserve the socio- cultural and economic identity of the people of Ri-Bhoi district; however it is also important to note that this predominantly tribal mode of lifestyle and productivity can no longer provide and sustain the people with adequate means of livelihood. A change from this traditional mode of lifestyle to a broader perspective is urgently needed if at all this society will be able to keep pace with the fast moving modern age. Hence the findings of the study reveal that the only way to promote the economic status of the people in the district is to bring about awareness, positive attitude, and sincere effort from the people themselves and an understanding of professionalism in their daily activities. Coupled with proper initiative and support from other quarters as mentioned earlier, surely bamboo shoot trade will enhance and work wonder in the livelihood of our villagers at Ri-Bhoi district and ensure them a sustainable and secure life.

Scenes From Ribhoi District

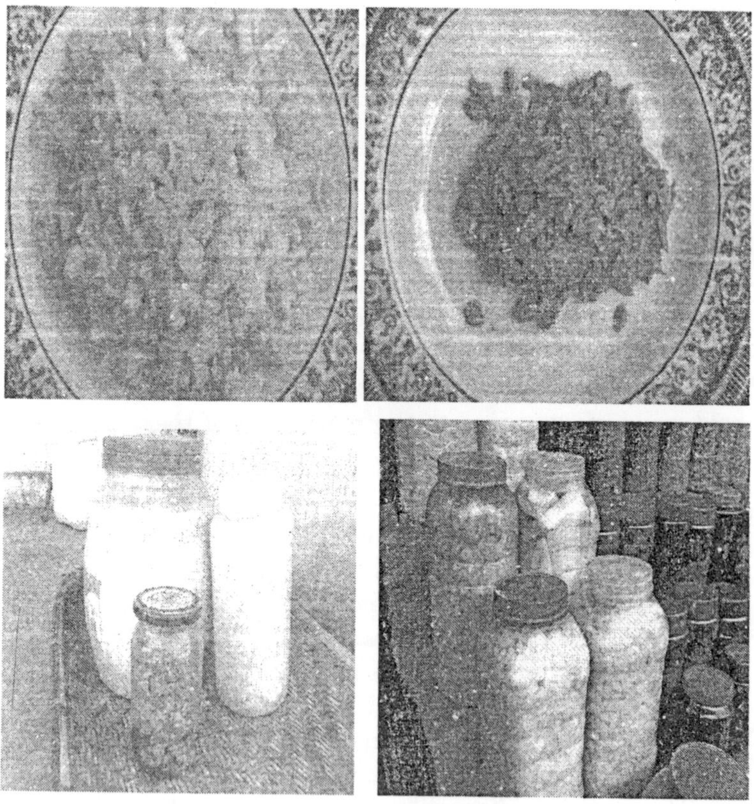

Acknowledgement

Sincere thanks goes to the Internal Quality Assurance Cell of Synod College, Shillong, which organized the National Seminar on the theme “Innovative Resourcing: Empowering Rural Livelihood”. Also our gratitude goes to the Principal of Synod College and the Coordinator IQAC for inviting and encouraging us to participate in the seminar. Last but not least we express our thanks and appreciation to all the participants, the office staffs, the computer lab, and the people of Ribhoi district who have help and supported us during our study of the region.]

REFERENCES

1. S.Khongsit *Hangne Tang Ia U Siej* Published: Mrs Swila Khongngain, Shynna Diengiei, San Mer Upper Shillong Shillong-793009.
2. Goverment of Meghalaya, *Ribhoi At A Glance, 2009* Office Of The District Statistical Officer Ribhoi District, Nongpoh
3. Goverment of Meghalaya, *Statistical Handbook,* Office of The District Statistical Officer Ribhoi District, 2009 Ribhoi District, Nongpoh
4. D.T. Zimba, *Geography of Meghalaya,* Text with Instant Notes Zimba Publications Maya Villa, Kench's Trace Bishnupur, Shillong- 793004
5. A.C. Mohapatra, S.K. Barik, C.S. Rao, *Man and Environmen* Second Enlarged 2000 Star Publishing House Shillong
6. Government of India, Meghalaya, Printing group of Survey of India East and West Khasi Hills District,1966-6767 Sheet no: 78 O/ 13, 78O/9, 83 B/4, 83C/15, 83 C/1, 78 K/1
7. R.C Tiwari *Geography of India* Second Revised Edition Prayag Pustak Bhawan, Allahabad, India.
8. Ministry of Environment and Forest, MOEF 1994.

7

Reallocation of Resources in Mountain Economies Applying DAE: A Case Study of Darjeeling Tea

Shubhro Michael Gomes

Introduction

The mountain economy is characterized as a rural economy. The empowerment of rural economies especially in the mountains has always been challenging. It requires an innovative effort. It is a notable fact that such economies have a history of isolation. There is a lack of in-depth research in this area. The present paper attempts to identify possible ways of reallocation of resources in an environment of collaboration of firms in a predominant industry in mountain economies. There are three sections of the paper. The first section discusses about various principal factors that have a bearing on mountain economies and have the potential of bringing about a change. The second section is on the case study. It discusses in brief about data envelopment analysis considered for the case study, objectives of the study, etc. The third section is conclusion and suggestions.

Factors Influencing Changes in Mountain Economies

The mountain economy as a rural economy has become quite important for its habitants as well as others. There are various principal factors, which are bound to leave an impact on it. Three factors, according to Soni and Kodali (2008) have been identified as principal factors, which have a bearing on the mountain economies:

Globalization

a) Global markets and competition will lead to changes in scope, scale and lead-time adding complexity in planning and execution.

b) Mixing culture and races affecting market profiles will change supply chain plans.

c) Production resources including skilled workers will be globally distributed even more, leading to higher lead-time and uncertainty.

d) Global democratization will lead to new markets, hence increasing complexity and lead-time.

e) SMEs (small marketing enterprises) will become part of global network, this will need organizational changes.

f) Global companies will be perceived as local and their growing size will require them to be self-governing and learning like a complex biological organism.

Information Technology

a) Betterment in knowledge sharing and communications will enhance competitive climate.

b) Market visibility and communications will rapidly improve to enhance speed of information flow and product traceability.

c) More real time applications and decision support systems will be required.

d) High connectivity of IT supported systems will make it possible to fulfill orders from various sources in real time, using virtual supply chains.

e) Advancement of IT will enable quicker organizational learning and knowledge.

Environmental Concerns

a) Persistent pressure to replenish natural resources by improving design and technology will need modifications in manufacturing and supplier base.

b) Regulatory norms on recycling will impact supply chain design.

c) Reverse logistics will be indispensable in supply chain decisions, which will involve issues such as product disassembly for reuse, remanufacturing, and product traceability.

d) Reduced dependence in natural resources will make supply chains more stable and sustainable.

e) Constant increase in pressure on supply chains to use environment-friendly materials in production, distribution, usage and disposal will affect production technologies and hence, the partners.

Case Study

The case study is based on tea industry in Darjeeling, a district of West Bengal, India. A sample of ten units is selected and four parameters have been considered for the study –

(a) Input variables:

(i) Number of requisitions on suppliers (S); and

(ii) Average number of employees on roll (W);

(b) Output variables:

(i) Number of export orders (E); and

(ii) Number of domestic orders (D);

Data Envelopment Analysis (DEA) is a multi-factor productivity analysis model for measuring the relative efficiencies of a homogenous set of DMUs (Talluri, 2000). DEA can be used to find out targets for units based on various parameters having effect on performance of companies, also known as Decision Making Units (DMUs), at the inter-company level.

The technical efficiencies (TE) have been calculated by using both the DEA models – Constant Returns to Scale (CRS) as well as Variable Returns to Scale (VRS). The DEAP version 1.2 has been used fir the present study.

The objective of the study is to attempt reallocation of resources and to identify possible gains from such reallocation. The study considered the application of DEA in two stages. The first stage DEA was applied to determine the targets and the second stage DEA was applied to make a comparative analysis of the two sets.

First Stage DEA

The results of the first stage DEA relating to efficiency scores of all the DMUs are presented in Table 1.

Table 1: Stage One Efficiency Summary

DMUs	*TECHNICAL EFFICIENCY*		*SCALE EFFICIENCY*	
	CRS DEA (CRSTE)	*VRS DEA (VRSTE)*	*SCALE = (CRSTE/VRSTE)*	*NATURE OF SCALE INEFFICIENCIES (RETURNS TO SCALE)*
1	0.593	1.000	0.593	DECREASING
2	0.936	1.000	0.936	DECREASING
3	0.452	0.602	0.751	DECREASING
4	1.000	1.000	1.000	CONSTANT
5	0.732	0.917	0.798	DECREASING
6	0.613	0.681	0.900	DECREASING
7	1.000	1.000	1.000	CONSTANT
8	0.764	0.831	0.919	DECREASING
9	1.000	1.000	1.000	CONSTANT
10	0.299	0.300	0.996	INCREASING
MEAN	0.739	0.833	0.889	

The above summary indicates the nature of inefficiencies

and where the individual DMUs are presently operating. For the purpose of benchmarking, the peer(s) were identified as in Table 2 along with their peer weights of the inefficient DMUs.

Table 2: Stage One Summary of Peers and Peer Weights

DMUs	*PEER 1*	*WEIGHTS*	*PEER 2*	*WEIGHTS*	*PEER 3*	*WEIGHTS*
3	7	1.000				
5	2	0.091	7	0.909		
6	7	1.000				
8	9	0.458	7	0.115	2	0.427
10	9	1.000				

The other DMUs did not have any peer(s). The benchmarking process helps to determine the revised targets – on the basis of projections of the inefficient DMUs 3, 5, 6, 8 and 10 so that they can improve themselves accordingly.

The output and input slack related to the DMUs have been presented in Graph 1.

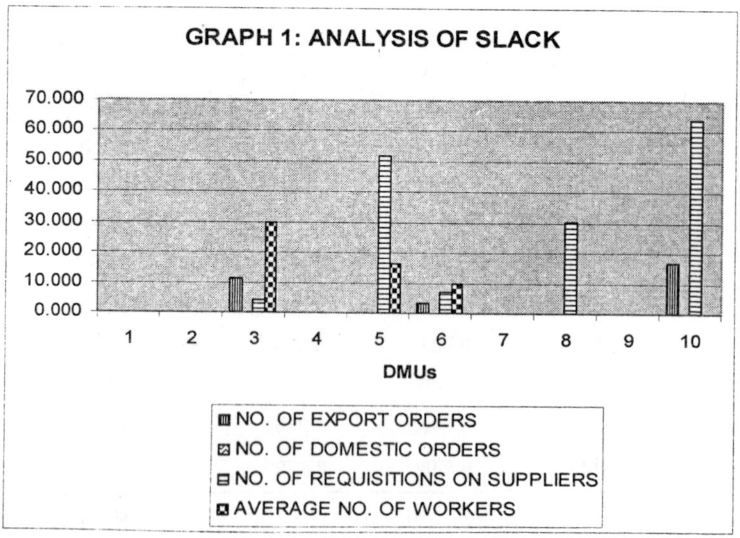

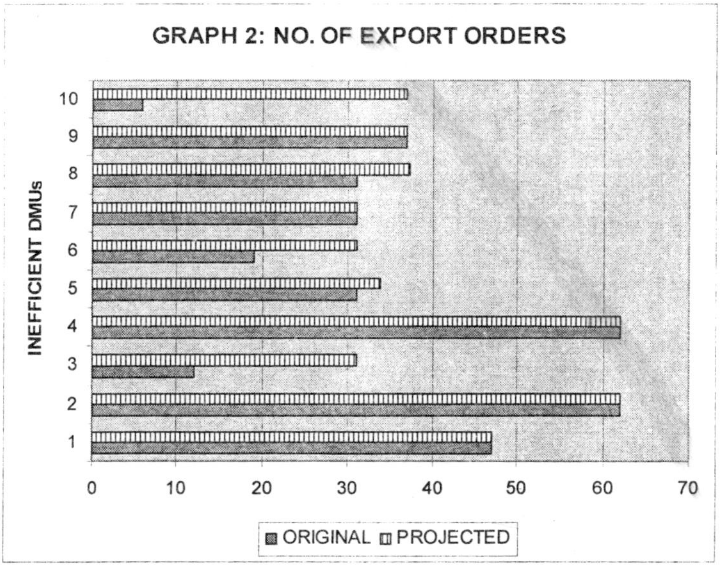

It is to be noted that the slack has been reported by those DMUs which are inefficient – DMUs 3,5,6,8 and 10.

On the basis of the analysis, projections for the output factor – number of export orders were made for the inefficient DMUs 3, 5, 6, 8 and 10 which has been graphically presented in Graph 2.

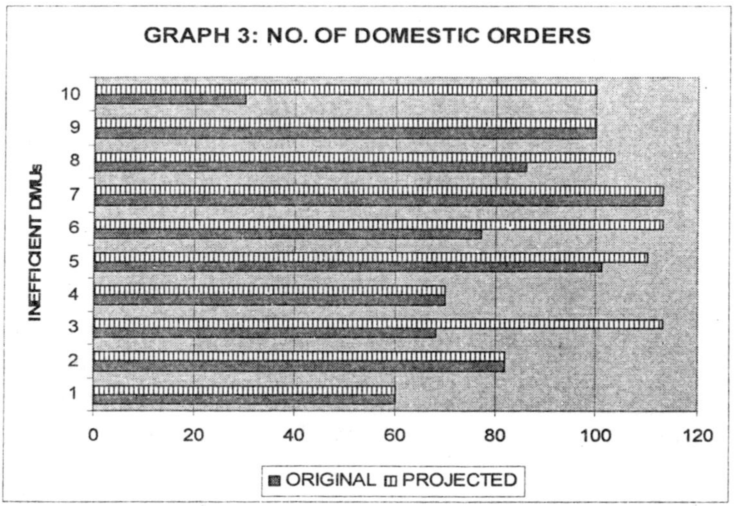

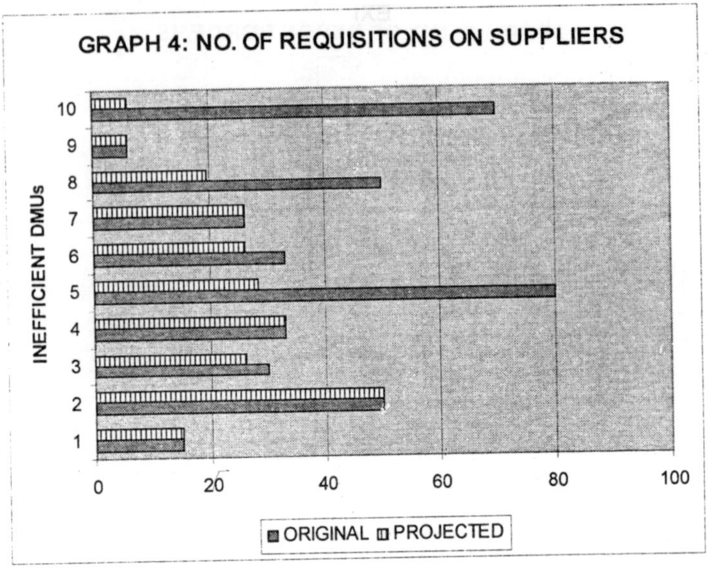

The graph reveals that DMUs 3,5,6,8 and 10 have to increase the number of export orders.

On the basis of the analysis, projections for the output factor – number of domestic orders were made for the inefficient DMUs 3, 5, 6, 8 and 10 which has been graphically presented in Graph 3.

The graph reveals that DMUs 3,5,6,8 and 10 have to increase the number of domestic orders.

On the basis of the analysis, projections for the input factor – number of requisitions on suppliers were made for the inefficient DMUs 3, 5, 6, 8 and 10 which has been graphically presented in Graph 4.

The graph reveals that DMUs 3,5,6,8 and 10 have to decrease the number of requisitions on suppliers.

On the basis of the analysis, projections for the input factor – average number of workers on rolls were made for the inefficient DMUs 3, 5, 6, 8 and 10 which has been graphically presented in Graph 5.

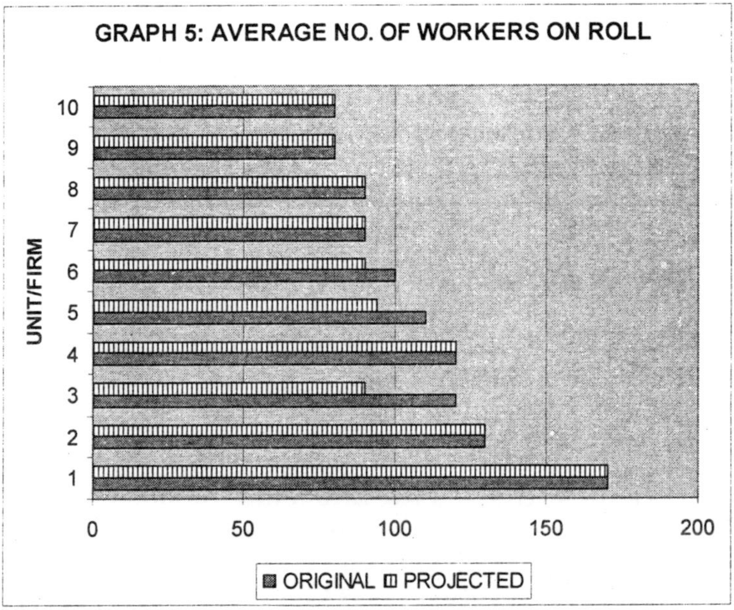

The graph reveals that DMUs 3, 5 and 6 have to decrease the average number of workers on roll.

Table 3: Targets for DMUs

DMU	*E*	*D*	*S*	*W*
1	47.000	60.000	15.000	170.000
2	62.000	82.000	50.000	130.000
3	31.000	113.000	26.000	90.000
4	62.000	70.000	33.000	120.000
5	33.818	110.182	28.182	93.636
6	31.000	113.000	26.000	90.000
7	31.000	113.000	26.000	90.000
8	37.304	103.487	19.582	90.000
9	37.000	100.000	6.000	80.000
10	37.000	100.000	6.000	80.000

Second Stage DEA

The firms/units (identified as inefficient DMUs) in the first stage are to redesign their plans and policies to achieve their targets and upon successful achievement, it is assumed that they will be able to sustain as well as enhance their performance. The target figures of the DMUs are given below in Table 3.

The targets figures are the reallocation of resources that can be applied. The DEA prescribes a particular target. It is more acceptable and perhaps desirable. Once these targets were ascertained, another DEA was performed and the results of the second stage DEA were found to be as below in Table 4:

Table 4: Stage Two Efficiency Summary

DMUs	*TECHNICAL EFFICIENCY*			*SCALE EFFICIENCY*
	CRS DEA (CRSTE)	*VRS DEA (VRSTE)*	*SCALE = (CRSTE/VRSTE)*	*NATURE OF SCALE INEFFICIENCIES (RETURNS TO SCALE)*
1	0.593	1.000	0.593	DECREASING
2	0.936	1.000	0.936	DECREASING
3	1.000	1.000	1.000	
4	1.000	1.000	1.000	
5	0.934	1.000	0.934	DECREASING
6	1.000	1.000	1.000	
7	1.000	1.000	1.000	
8	0.915	0.994	0.921	DECREASING
9	1.000	1.000	1.000	
10	1.000	1.000	1.000	
MEAN	0.938	0.999	0.938	

The above results also indicate that there is a possibility of enhancing the performance. This is evident from the fact as presented in Table 5.

Table 5: Comparative Statement

TECHNICAL EFFICIENCY			*SCALE EFFICIENCY*
STAGE	*CRS DEA (CRSTE)*	*VRS DEA (VRSTE)*	*SCALE = (CRSTE/VRSTE)*
1	0.739	0.833	0.889
2	0.938	0.999	0.938
CHANGE	+26.93%	+19.93%	+5.51%

There will be an overall change – an increment in this case.

It will also help sustain and enhance the performance of the Darjeeling region. It is important to note that it is not a one-time exercise. The whole process should be reviewed and repeated on a regular basis – to aim at continuous enhancement efforts through on-going benchmarking. This is evident from the fact as presented in Table 6 below:

Table 6: Stage Two Summary of Peers and Peer Weights

DMUs	*PEER 1*	*WEIGHTS*	*PEER 2*	*WEIGHTS*	*PEER 3*	*WEIGHTS*
6	3	1.000				
7	3	1.000				
8	2	0.113	3	0.435	9	0.452
10	9	1.000				

Thus, it is evident that an on-going effort is required a further enhancement is possible. This is because the entire set of firms will be measured and compared at a new level of operations.

Conclusion and Suggestions

In the present paper an attempt has been made to reallocate the resources that are scarce in order to enhance performance. The above facts indicate that it is possible. It is now left to the players to decide whether they want to excel or not. There are certain limitations of DEA – it is deterministic and particularly sensitive to measurement errors. However, it can guide the players to benchmark their as well as their partners' performance. This paper also suggest that the owners of tea gardens, tea distributors and those related can form supply chains and participate in benchmarking exercises towards sustainable performance. It is always to be noted that an ongoing effort is advisable in order to achieve the true gains.

REFERENCES

Forrester, J. W. (1958) Industrial dynamics: A major breakthrough for decision makers. *Harvard Business Review*, July/August, 37-66.

Charnes A., Cooper, W.W. and Rhodes, E., (1978), Measuring Efficiency of Decision-making Units, *European Journal of Operational Research*, 2, 429-444.

Meyer, M. (1997) The performance imperative, Unpublished Working Paper, University of Pennsylvania, Philadelphia.

Talluri, Srinivas, (2000), Data Envelopment Analysis: Models and Extensions, *Decision Line*, pp.8-11.

Soni, G and Kodali, R (2008) Evolution of Supply Chain Management: Developments in Academia and Industry, *The ICFAI Journal of Supply Chain Management*, Vol. V, No. 4, December 2008

http://www.uq.edu.au/economics/cepa/software.htm

8

Confronting Ethnic & Social Barriers to Micro Development Resourcing in Northeast India

A. DeCruz

Introduction

India's Northeast has long been characterized by insurgent conflict, political agitation, and economic unrest. As a result, the impact of development efforts in this region has been inconclusive. In terms of the different government-run and non-governmental approaches to microfinance, there is a call for researcher and practitioner to collaborate. As to whether liberal economic development has impacted communitarian livelihoods at all, analysis of the data remains inconclusive. For the sake of the national and worldwide microfinance community, new study data and observations on North-eastern MFIs should be documented. To serve that end, this paper unwraps the anomalous, grassroots-level experience of one MFI to transcend borders in a vast and one of the most culturally divergent regions of the world. What conventions and adaptations result offer versed perspective into an undocumented sector of microfinance—overcoming cultural and ethnic trade barriers in the tribal Northeast.

This paper on the efforts of the Society for Micro Economy Development Activities (SoFMEDA) in Shillong, Meghalaya. By detailing the methodology of the group's various innovative approaches to ethnic, geographic, and cultural obstacles, the greater microfinance community may gain perspective to lending in Northeast India: regionally, to development in the Northeast states of India; and universally, to cultural identity conflicts that frustrate the call for microfinance. This paper will detail key innovative approaches used by SoFMEDA with regard to resource mobilization: employing a diversified staff, using the ethnic and social backgrounds of those staff to attend to client's needs and problems and mobilizing the church to access social networks. Additionally, it will cover problems SoFMEDA faces and responses to them.

In order to organize the approaches and perspectives of this paper, we will begin by framing an outline of the unrest in the Northeast with information specific to micro lenders. We present a second, necessary premise, which functions to illustrate the NGO—its background, policy framework, and loan schemes. From there we will also discuss the society's tactics to accommodate myriad ethnic groups in the region and methods to overcome geographic barriers.

Organizational Framework

Background of SoFMEDA's Environment, Beginnings, and Structural Policy

Northeast India

Bordering Myanmar, China, Bhutan, and Bangladesh, the Northeast consists of eight sister states (Sikkim being the latest state to be included into its fold) geographically isolated from mainland India except by an approximately 20-kilometer-wide strip of land. Because of its location, the land is home to many immigrants and refugees from surrounding nations. As a cultural epicentre, it hosts over 200 tribal groups, each with unique cultures; and in addition, there is a plurality of diverse languages and dialects.

SoFMEDA Background

The US-based non-profit, World Relief planted the idea for SoFMEDA in 1994, which began as a micro-credit assistance program in partnership with and under the direction of the North East India Committee on Relief and Development (NEICORD). However, the society did not take shape until March of 1995 when NEICORD authorized the project as a program under their name. Prior to formal lending, the group disbursed five loans experimentally under a self-help scheme. During that time, a third organization – the Evangelical Fellowship of India Commission on Relief (EFICOR) – offered consultation. Together the efforts of a multinational, a development agency, and a consulting group set the foundation of the trans-state developmental society.

Only the most basic tenets of policy carried the organization in its infancy. Step-by-step, the program crafted a more structured approach. Upon the success of the first five groups, the assistance program expanded, but gradually. Growth was both progressive and reactive; the group added new policy measures only as needed. The elements constituting SoFMEDA's policy and regiment today result from years of gradual accumulation—compiled from an attentive willingness to correct mistakes. From 200 clients in 1996 to over 8,000 in 2009, each step of progress was ordained by BOARD-sanctioned approval. As it refers to this study, innovations outlined in this paper are current as of 31st, July 2009.

Geographic Expansion and Positioning of SoFMEDA

After a successful cycle of pilot tests in 1994, SoFMEDA extended services to Manipur in 1995. By early 1997, the credit assistance program emerged as an independent organization with a separate office and formal identity under the Societies Registration Act. By 1998, the program extended hands to Mizoram; by 2001, Nagaland; and by 2002, Tripura. Today, SoFMEDA provides financial services in the states of

Assam, Manipur, Mizoram, and Meghalaya from a single field office in Shillong, Meghalaya. As an independent, not-for profit NGO, SoFMEDA is a registered society under the government of Meghalaya. Its only remaining formal partner is World Relief.

Basic Organizational Structure[1]

SoFMEDA currently has over fifteen Promoters who coordinate the micro-credit program at the grassroots level, and are in constant contact with all group leaders. The word promoter is SoFMEDA vernacular for field worker. They are responsible for forming groups, monitoring clients, and collecting repayments. Depending on the number of clients under their oversight, Promoters' status as staff of SoFMEDA ranges from volunteer to full-time, and they are compensated accordingly. In terms of contact, delinquency-assistance, and authority, the Promoters are directly accountable to Project Officers.

Project Officers work in the office, and initiate, implement, and monitor programs. These individuals are also responsible for tracking clients, making reports, and for coordinating activities in the designated regions. Project Officers are accountable to the Executive Director, who in turn is responsible to the Board of Directors.

Credit Programme

SoFMEDA seeks an approach to microfinance that reaches poor, often displaced individuals and families throughout Northeast India. The hope is that not only each participant be empowered to a higher standard of living through holistic transformation, but that the family, as an extension of the client, is impacted as well. To assess client eligibility, SoFMEDA maintains conventional regulations. The target group may consist of young men and women considered economically as active poor (with an annual household income below Rs.60,000/-, and are part of minority or tribal groups. These economically active poor clients often do not have the ability to borrow funds from commercial banks, forcing them into the hands of moneylenders, which is a serious ramification of the lack of micro finance institutions (MFIs) in the Northeast. Target clients should be between 18-65 years of age and demonstrate a sense of entrepreneurial and team spirit. To date, 98% of SoFMEDA's clients are women.

SoFMEDA works through the formation of self-help groups (SHGs), which are self-initiated (by interested clients) and sustained by the 5 to 20 members.[2] SHG regulations are defined per the Reserve Bank of India, and are either registered or unregistered with the Indian government.

Loan Scheme

Before availing a loan, members must possess individual savings of a minimum Rs.500. Loan amounts per client start at Rs. 4000/- followed by a 2nd cycle of Rs.6000, a 3rd of Rs.8000, a 4th of Rs.10000, a 5th of Rs.12000, and a final, 6th cycle of Rs.15000.[3] After completing 6 cycles, a client should have invested a total of Rs.55000 in a business. Loan repayment is simple; every loan is paid back in 10 equal monthly payments with 1.5% operational cover charge.[4] Over the course of 10 months the client will have paid a 1.5% monthly interest, which amounts to 15% interest paid on the overall loan. In the case that a client defaults, the self-help group (SHG) is required to cover the delinquent member's missed repayments. That is, members of a group guarantee one another's loans, which they agree to at the time of application.

Mobilizing Human Resources

Overcoming Cultural Boundaries with Local Staff

In the Northeast as in any part of the world, one might conjecture that racial tensions exist as a result of social and political histories. Some cultural barriers to trade may hinge on the assumptions that ethnic people groups make of one another. Because of the divisive nature of this topic, the sections titled *Staff Languages And Ethnology* and *Using Diverse Staff to Professionally attend to Clients Needs and Problems*, however, necessitate a premise that intergroup relations among peoples *may* be influenced by and vary as a result of ethnicity. This is important to keep in mind in the following section. Minding this stipulation accurately and constructing a statement around this premise requires both a profound understanding of clients' cultures and a grasp of clients' languages. At best, this section entails a look, albeit lacking an exhaustive reading, into measures that concern finance in the Northeast as an area with a thick social fabric and an immense ethnic backdrop which underline social situations involved in the business and lending process. Therefore, the following sections are meant to explain innovations in microfinance with respect to race and ethnicity, but without imposing a racial agenda or making assumptions of one or any particular tribal people group.

Staff Languages and Ethnology

Relational gaps in inter-tribal relations may pervade business activities. What we mean by this is that different cultural or ethnic backgrounds can result in miscommunication. Clients are weary to avail a loan especially when they don't have the encouragement of someone from their own tribe as an example success story. Take for example a client from the Hmar tribe in the Northeast talking with a promoter or loan officer, also Hmar. That client is far more likely to feel confident taking a loan, given the risk, when someone of similar background has availed a loan successfully.

The idea here is that clients may find it encouraging when a person of their own native tribe or tongue has been successful. Therefore, SoFMEDA enlists a diversified group of staff members. In the field and in the office, SoFMEDA employee ethnicities represent the predominant tribes of the region. Also, loan officers generally oversee the region from which they originated or have kin. Additionally, it is by measure of policy that promoter and client speak the same language. Among seven office employees, 19 languages are represented, 7 of which are spoken fluently. Among field staff, additional languages may be present. Before entering new regions where clients of unreached tribes live, SoFMEDA recruits a promoter from that location to oversee future loan activity in the area.

Using Diverse Staff to Professionally attend to Clients Needs and Problems

In microfinance, identifying with someone ethnically is important for client-to-lender relations. When delinquency occurs, clients express a need to feel identified with or understood. This need may be fulfilled when clients feel they can relate on a cultural level. For example, clients may feel more comfortable explaining their problems to someone from their like background. SoFMEDA's projects are managed by staffs whose cultural affinity is closely linked with the client's ethnicity. The payoff in this proposed solution is that clients display increased sense of ownership and responsibility toward their business as well as eagerness to repay loans. Therefore, by having an ethnically similar loan officer addressing their needs and problems, clients better understand the responsibilities and seriousness involved in taking a loan, which helps SoFMEDA more effectively target a solution. Ultimately, this is one way SoFMEDA can combat a cultural hindrance to microfinance at an interethnic relations level.

Of course, mobilizing local and diverse staff is intuitive; micro lenders themselves are often local to their region in which they set up business. This is common among MFIs in the Northeast. But from the international perspective, mobilizing indigenous human resources is vital. What can be gained from SoFMEDA's approach to use ethnically heterogeneous staff sheds light on the role played by ethnicity in business and its impact on micro financial practice.

Geographic Barriers

Mobilizing Existing Institutions in Tribal Vicinities

Understanding microfinance in the Northeast requires a working knowledge of its diverse geographic variance. The role that this plays in lending is self-evident. Any MFI that crosses national or political borders will have employees, at some level, working in the field. No matter the type of communication technology used, the region's geography will determine, impact, and regulate it. In this section, geographic variability will be discussed first as it relates to how it impedes the work of SoFMEDA (with respect to the means of communication); and second, how SoFMEDA has adapted to it.

Geographic Barriers to Lending in Northeast India

Backdropping geographic variability is the immense breadth of the Northeast, covering some 254,000 square miles;[5] whereas SoFMEDA operates in four of its seven states, these four states constitute 54.72%[6] of the geographic area of the Northeast. The terrain ranges from plains to riverbeds to hills to jungles. No matter the distance, transportation seems to be encumbered by poor road conditions. Evidence abounds that road conditions are of the foremost hindrances to trade in Northeast India. Take for instance clients living in jungles, where roads may not exist at all. Or in other terrains, where not only are roads precarious and seasonal, but many are unpaved and dependent on the weather. In terms of government oversight, roads are not well maintained, but rather neglected which makes roadway environments haphazard and dangerous. Further exacerbating the inefficiency of travel is insurgency, which ushers in bandhs, roadblocks, and other travel dilemmas. Also, many village communities are isolated from one another.

Impacts of Geographic Barriers on SoFMEDA

The impact of geographic conditions is twofold: 1) it

becomes difficult to locate new clients; and 2) more generally, staff-to-client relations suffer as a result. Because our focus is innovation, we will neglect to detail the latter point to avoid redundancy. The former will be the focus of this section to offer novelty and perspective to the microfinance community.

Finding New Clients

Finding new clients may be the greatest obstacle to expansion for MFIs in Northeast India because many communities are geographically isolated from one another. As a result, communities become socially disconnected. To locate clients in hard-to-reach areas and to assess the feasibility of lending, SoFMEDA uses an approach called a *New Area Survey*. To perform the survey, SoFMEDA observes and rates the integrity of local infrastructure and phone networks, the number of post offices and banks, and the level of accessibility to the potential region.

Methodology of the New Area Survey

When SoFMEDA seeks new clients, the process begins in the office. Project officers deliberate with the executive director and suggest possible sites. After reaching a consensus, the group sends one project officer to perform the *New Area Survey* in person.

The next step is to contact a church. Though surveying is important for data collection, pinpointing a church contact is more. Contact is made in person or over the phone, where the project officer pitches the mission, vision, and background information of SoFMEDA.

The process can take several months. After making the presentation to the local community, clients form SHGs and fill out loan applications. Before reviewing applications, SoFMEDA proposes to the board the feasibility of extending loans to the target community. Upon approval, applications are reviewed and the loan process begins.

Why Use the Church as a Resource?

One of the greatest setbacks to the Northeast is that geographic variance causes many dissimilar tribal groups to live in close proximity. Of times, new clients are reached through the social networks of existing clients. When social circles are isolated linguistically and culturally, reaching new clients is difficult. There is a need, then, for a unifying theme among social networks. One unifying theme SoFMEDA has observed is the widespread impact of Christianity on tribal peoples in the Northeast. This spread of Christian ideology is unique to the character of the Northeast region. Its expanding influence functions as a unifying social medium among SoFMEDA's diverse clientele. For this reason, SoFMEDA uses local churches as a tool to get a foothold in regional networks, especially in remote tribal vicinities.

The idea that, through churches, a MFI can access a social network with ideological (and perhaps social) commonality is, to some extent, original, and may have the affect of targeting clients who are encouraged to make ethical decisions. As a MFI who collects no collateral and gives out financially unsecured loans, SoFMEDA relies on the integrity of clients to uphold their commitment to repaying the loans. Boosting the integrity of clients will positively affect the outcome of administering loans.

The idea of using churches is like mobilizing existing development in an underdeveloped area. In underdeveloped areas, one doesn't go building new roads or founding banks if they are already present. One should use whatever resources are available. If there is a post office, use it for field correspondence; a bank, use its secured deposits; a commodity business, use its resources to buy capital; a social gathering, use its contacts. In the same way, if easy-to-access social networks exist in a region, lenders should make use of those resources. For this reason, the local church is a means to tapping new social networks.

Conclusion

Seeking to be an effective micro lender in Northeast India has created many challenges. Several geographic and ethnic barriers inherent in the Northeast region have created added difficulties in lending. To counteract these issues, SoFMEDA has used a set of two specific innovations; these include mobilizing a diverse staff and empowering them strategically and using the church as gateway to new clients in large social networks.

REFERENCES

1. Thanabalan, Matthew. *Impact Assessment: Society for Micro Economy Development Activities.* July 2008.
2. Society for Micro Economy Development Activities. *Credit Policy.* August 2009.
3. NEHU Library. *Developmental Issues of North-East India*

NOTES

1 Society for Micro Economy Development Activities

- Credit Policy
- August 2009.

2 Thanabalan, Matthew. *Impact Assessment: Society for Micro Economy Development Activities.* July 2008.

3 Society for Micro Economy Development Activities

- Credit Policy
- August 2009.

4 Thanabalan, Matthew. *Impact Assessment: Society for Micro Economy Development Activities.* July 2008.

5 NEHU Library. Developmental Issues of North-East India

6. NEHU Library. Developmental Issues of North-East India (Numbers added my own from table)

9

Empowering Rural Women Through Distance Education

Ratan Lal Godara & S.M.Gomes

Introduction

In distance learning, most of the women share goals and ambitions similar to those of students in the conventional education system. This means that they are seeking degrees for a number of reasons including economic career advancement, higher wages and individual development. They take up vocations and skills for personal fulfillment by obtaining a degree or by gaining useful knowledge to fulfill personal or social goals. They are searching for knowledge as well as a sense of achievement that this offers. (Evans 1995, Furst-Bowe 2001).

When selecting a distance-learning program, in addition to considering the nature of the degree and the type of delivery system, women students consider several general factors including the programme availability and quality, the institutional reputation and its location, the service quality and costs (Furst-Bowe 2001, Mowen and Parks 1997). Furthermore, more number of adult women students selected a distance learning program because of the way it fits in with the other demands of their lives. As far as the selected courses are concerned, women choose to enroll in greater proportions in arts, human studies and social sciences. It seems that despite the development of technology over the past decade and the emphasis on computer skills within the school curriculum, (Lockwood 1995), "the belief continues to persist that females are by nature technologically ignorant and unable to absorb scientific and technological information or to acquire technical skills" (Deligianni-Kouimtzi and Zioogou 1993, Fragkoudaki 1985).

Women in Rural India

In Indian context, rural women empowerment is very essential through distance education. Hence, one can look into the following features of rural women status in India. In India rural women suffer with respect to various causes and reasons. They are: (i) marginality of attention and services of rural women in rural and agricultural development (ii) special constraints to their development and lack of training to develop their awareness and skills, lack of information and lack of bargaining power (iii) low productivity and narrow occupational choice (iv) inadequate finance and expert guidance for promoting socio-economic activity of rural women and their participation (v) inadequate monitoring of women's participation (vi) inadequate application of science and technology to remove drudgery and (vii) low health and nutritional status.

Majority of women in general and rural women in particular have access to education particularly higher education in the formal system. Hence, there is a growing realization on women empowerment through distance mode of education. It has been realised on account of many factors. Hence, there is a need to discuss this problem in the present situation. Social empowerment is one of the aspects of women development. It envisages women to have equal status along with encouraging participation and power of decision making at the household and also at the community level since the majority of the rural women are denied their rights and privileges. Social empowerment could be achieved by overcoming social, cultural and religious barriers. It is also essential to achieve equality of status and recognition of women in their day to day affairs and on matters concerning them. Moreover, social empowerment aims at increasing the status of women in terms of participation and decision making process in democratic institutions.

The second aspect of rural women development is economic empowerment. It could be achieved in the form of greater access to financial resources outside the household, reducing vulnerability of poor women to crisis situation like famine, food, riots, accidents etc. in the family. Hence, there is a need to increase the level of rural women's income and the power to retain such income and use it at their discretion. Further, economic empowerment should be assured in the form of equal access and control over various resources at the household level and also financial self-reliance of women both in the household and in the external environment. Capacity building is one of the aspects of developing rural women. The capacity building depends on better awareness of health, education, environment, legal rights and improvement of functional literacy and numeracy. It also includes better communication skills, better leadership skills and self-help and mutual help. Thus achievement of overall women empowerment depends on distance education particularly school dropouts among rural women and the Open University system also promotes education for semi-literate rural women. However, many factors hinder education of rural women by distance mode.

Barriers to Educating Rural Women Through Distance Education

Any learning at any age requires time, space and support. At a distance, the onus is on the learner to organize the necessary space structure and their available time, these often accompanied by external and internal conflicts. These are conflicts related to a series of corresponding barriers whose relative significance varies according to the level of education and training, the age of the women and the cultural context. (Evans 1995). Further to this point, we put forward the barriers to women's participation in distance learning; barriers which are underpinned by contemporary ideological and social structures. Improving the indicators that concern the participation of women in distance learning will succeed if only the educational institutions comprehend these obstacles. Despite the high enrollment rates, a large percentage of female students drop out before completing the program for non-academic reasons. (Furst-Bowe, 2001).

Even though they try hard to combine study with other responsibilities, and despite the motivation and dedication, many are still made to feel that they are letting their families down when they try to extend further their education. (Kramarae 2000) Distance learning demands devotion and time and there are male partners who experience anxiety owing to the extent that they are alienated from this new concern for women's lives. Tolerance is conditional based on length of time spent and potential neglect of relationships and responsibilities, but on the understanding that this is an aberration. Some women feel obliged to "pay back" this tolerance through restricting time spent and normalizing relationships. (Burke 2000).

Dowling (1983) argues that the fear of women achieving success leads them to choices beneath their possibilities and generally hinders their social development. "It seems as if women are consumed by "gendered panic" in the face of success", she points out. One can assume the consequences that this attitude will have on women's self-esteem and confidence (Nova 1994) and evidently on their studies, especially in the distance learning mode, where initiative plays a decisive role.

For all the benefits of distance learning for women, these students still have to make tremendous sacrifices to balance the demands of work, family, and school study, writing assignments, research etc. as mothers, female partners, employees and citizens. That is why the majority of women declare anxiety, and many others especially mothers of young children often do their coursework while the other family members are sleeping (Morgan 1991, Stalker 1997, May 1994) commented that taking on distance study roles often results in "double duty" and Kramarae (2000) concludes that working mothers interested in further studies are adding a difficult "third shift" to their responsibilities. "We need to deal with the time bind that all parents and older students face if we want to make the rhetoric of "lifelong learning" for the "information economy" a reality", she suggests.

Women empowerment depends on access to education. However, rural women do not have easy access to education due to various causes and reasons. This section makes a comprehensive discussion about factors hindering women's access to distance education.

Common patterns in lack of family support for women engaged in distance learning are the cultural and cross-cultural social norms and traditions by which the subservient status of women is maintained. (Effeh 1991, Kirkup and Abbot 1997, Athanasiadou 2002). However, the intersection of discourses at home is located where traditional and postmodern gender expectations collide. The under education of women due to cultural restrictions at their expense, not only in developing countries (Commonwealth Secretariat 1987), but in many developed countries (United Nations 2000, Vergidis 1995) is one more limiting factor since it deprives women of the basic prerequisite necessary for distance learning studies. The principle of the autonomy of the programme participants with their interaction and the teaching material, as well as the development of critical thinking abilities, that are applied in distance learning, create additional problems of adaptation in women who follow the general model of passivity of their gender. (Evans 1995, May 1994).

As feminists have pointed out for decades, when women pursue an interest or activity which does not relate directly to their domestic role, and effectively expose and challenge unequal power relations within the family, they quite often meet with strong resistance from male partners because of suspicion/jealousy as well as ridicule. (Evans 1995). Sometimes wider family with children, parents and parents-in-law, creates and sustains internal and external barriers to study, reinforcing gender stereotypes. Greek grandmothers who do baby-sitting during the face-to-face Team Counseling meetings usually state, "She should be at home taking care of her family. What does she want with this course of action?"

In general majority of the rural households are either illiterate or semi-literate. In such households there is no self-interest on the part of women members. This is due to lack of knowledge and awareness of education. Hence efforts should be made to develop self-motivation among rural women with a view to give them educational opportunities by distance education mode.

In rural India, majority of the poor households are unable to meet their basic needs. In this situation they send their female children as wage labour rather than to school. They feel double burden with respect to educating their female children; it is loss of earning due to sending female children to school and the second one is the cost of educating their children. Thus supplementing household income as wage labour prevents women's education by distance mode.

In rural area because of illiteracy and semi-illiteracy majority of the rural households do not know anything about existing opportunities and potentialities and ways and means of availing themselves of such opportunities. Further due to lack of communication they do not know about available courses, subjects, degrees, diplomas etc., by distance education. Hence efforts should be made about possible ways and means of continuing their education by distance mode.

Further difficulties may present themselves in lessons that demand the extended use of computers for example. (Furst-Bowe 2001, May 1994). Due to the fact that women may have (whether they believe or not) less ease of use and experience working with technological interfaces. Female students may have less experience of working with technology than do their male counterparts and may become frustrated with distance learning courses that require extensive use of computers. Despite, they belief that females are by nature technologically ignorant and unable to absorb scientific and technological information or acquire technical skills. One more obstacle related to the nature of distance learning programs is that students experience isolation and lack of individual attention. The sense of isolation that women students experience in their studies is due to the lack of natural contact with their peers (Kirkup and Von Prummer 1990, Furst-Bowe 2001). Gilligan (1982) confirms the difference of women, supporting that the tendency of women to share their studies with their classmates, their friends and their families is not connected to any type of inferiority or to any negative personal experiences, but to a positive stance of participation and "dependent connection." This stance probably extends from their social role that strengthens a model of behaviour, which is less independent. (Beauvoir 1989).

In rural areas people are conservatives and their traditional background hinders their learning environment. Women in rural areas engage themselves in various households' activities and they find little time to engage themselves in reading and writing activities. Usually there is a discouraging social setup with regard to women's education. In illiterate and semi-illiterate households early marriage practice is quite common among women and it is a discouraging learning environment.

In villages people have gender bias towards girls' education. As a result, parents give more importance to educating their sons rather than daughters. Usually their daughters will be married of as soon as they attain puberty.

Tuition fees in distance learning are very expensive in some countries. It is obvious that the high cost of the studies inevitably hinders women's participation. This is a crucial factor especially for those who depend on their family for financial support or on sponsorship from their employers. Even women who have their own source of income are on an average paid less than their male counterparts, and as a result the economic obligations for study become insurmountable.

There are some other factors hindering education of rural women. They are listed here: Priority consideration for the education of male children in the household budget; Child labour practice; Uneducated peer group; Inadequate transport facility; High rate of dropouts at the primary level; Long distance of access to educational institutions Playing multiple roles etc.

Scholarships, the low tuition costs and the widening of economic assistance for distance learning study programmes are extended to the educational institutions and the state can make it easier for women with economic dependence to break free of social and educational isolation. The establishment of more local study centers is one way to counter the isolation that women distance learners' experience (thus ensuring a quiet place for study - supportive services and one-on-one lessons). (Effeh 1991) Educational policy-makers must be sensitized to the needs in particular of working mothers who are engaged in distance learning programmes. The services for the professional orientation, finally, belong to that category of supportive mechanisms which give meaning to all of the previous effort. Otherwise, there exists the strong possibility that women distance learners will be unable to utilize the knowledge and skills that are gained through the programme thus rendering their efforts futile both typically and essentially.

Professors and counselors can decisively contribute to the removal of barriers that women in distance learning encounter by treating distance learners as responsible and intelligent human beings, not as passive educational consumers (Kramarae 2000) and by creating a safe and supportive environment in accordance with the principles of adult education (Rogers 1999), with the intent of dispelling women's fears concerning education. Educators need to be sensitive to women's personal and unique circumstances and to investigate ways to help students develop effective support systems. Supportive conditions, which raise the self-confidence and self-awareness of the learner in the context of distance learning education, can be ensured by the use of a variety of communication means and pedagogical methods - strategies as well as the promotion of interaction between students, professors- counselors and technology. (Furst-Bowe 2001, Kirkup and VonPrummer 1990).

In order to promote distance learning education, the broad dissemination of information to women populations that can benefit from the advantages of distance learning programs of study but for whom it would be impossible otherwise to access the typical sources of information such as websites, must be ensured. Within this category are included unemployed women, older women, women living in rural/ agricultural areas, and women in prison. Women themselves can contribute to this effort through the network of women's movement and of women's professional organizations.

Discrimination against women must be confronted more generally. This means that parental prototypes must be changed that assign to women the bulk of child care (important here is the role of the mass media), and at least the legal provision of dependable - specialized and economic childcare during the course of study and of work for parents.

Educational institutions that provide distance-learning education must recognise that student learning environments comprise the home and local center from which women study as well as the educational institutions itself. First and foremost, the role that the house and the local setting play in the learning environment of the woman student must be recognised and the fact that this education, like technology must be adapted to local circumstances (May 1994). The next step is to conduct research into the special way in which women engage themselves in distance learning, into the types and levels of interaction between students and tutors that suit the female way of learning, as well as the documentation of the major social aspects that influence women's learning.

As far as the programme of study is concerned, more women's studies courses must be made available via distance learning programmes and a feminist perspective must be incorporated in the curriculum in other disciplines. More women administrators, teachers and students should be involved in the planning process for on-line courses so that their experience can contribute more directly to the benefit of others. (Kramarae 2000). This means that the possibility of adapting study programmes to suit the needs of women can be utilised in such a way that steadily the educational demands of other categories of learners can also be satisfied.

Strategies to Educating Rural Women Through Distance

In order to overcome the problems as cited above, one needs some action oriented programmes.

1. Conducting awareness campaign in rural areas, thereby the importance of women's education could be imparted to the rural households.
2. Involving women voluntary groups and non-governmental organisations to initiate various kinds of activities, which would motivate girls to go for higher education by distance mode.
3. There is a need to motivate women's self-help groups in imparting awareness of women's education through distance mode with a view to disseminate the same to their members.
4. Initiating special counseling programme on raising the study skills of women including career guidance in rural area itself.
5. There is a need to start rural communication centre with

a view to disseminate knowledge of educational opportunities available through distance education system.

6. Encouraging Open University system of learning among rural women. This can be done with the help of NGOs and civil society.
7. There is a need to reduce the cost of distance education, particularly for the benefit of rural women.
8. Universities should conduct awareness campaign in rural areas about the educational opportunities, courses offered, eligibility conditions etc. This will motivate rural women to pursue higher education by distance education.
9. School dropouts among rural girls should be encouraged to pursue their education by distance education system.
10. There is a need to impart computer education in rural Girls schools with a view to develop their vocational skills and thereby make use of them like IT in distance education.
11. Efforts should be made to enroll more girls' students under distance education system by offering job-oriented courses.
12. There is a need to start development programme to promote awareness of the academic needs of the rural women students.
13. The curriculum of distance education at least should have one general paper on women development, focusing on health and family welfare, environment awareness, plan policies and programmes pertaining to women empowerment.
14. There is a need to start separate website on courses offered by various universities under distance education system. The website address could be disseminated to our rural people particularly, girls and women.

REFERENCES

Athanasiadou K (2002). *Women in University education and the reconciliation of professional and family life.* Doctoral thesis, Department of Psychology, Thessaloniki.

Baig Tara Ali, (1976). India's *Women power* S. Chand , Co New Delhi

Beauvoir S (1989) *The Second Sex.* H. M. Parshley (Translator) Vintage Books'; Reissued Edition.

Burke C (2000) *Time and Space for Women: Distance Learning and Domestic Constraints,* School of Education, Bretton Hall College, UK.

Commonwealth Secretariat (1987) *Gender Stereotyping in Science, Technology and Mathematics Education.* Report of Commonwealth Africa Regional Workshop, Ghana.

Deligianni-Kouimtzi B and Ziogou S (1993) *Education and Gender.* Vanias Publications, Thessaloniki.

Dowling C (1983) *The Cinderella Complex.* Glaros Publications, Athens.

Effeh E (1991) Determinants of the study patterns of female distance learners: An evaluative survey. *Journal of Distance Education,* vol 6, no 2, pp. 58-63.

Evans K (1995) Distance Education: Helping overcome the barriers to women's technological education. *In the COL's (The Commonwealth of Learning) News Publication,* vol 6, no 2.

Fragoudaki A (1985) *Sociology and Education - Theories on the social inequality of school.* Papazizi Publications, Athens.

Furst-Bowe J (2001) *Identifying the Needs of Adult Women Learners in Distance Education Programs.* University of Wisconsin-Stout.

Gilligan C (1982) *In a different voice: Psychological theory and women's development.* Cambridge, MA, Harvard University Press.

Kirkup G and Abbott J (1997) *The Gender Gap: A Gender Analysis of the 1996 Computing Access Survey.* PLU, Milton Keynes.

Kramarae, Ch (2000) *The Third Shift: Women Learning* On-line, American Association of University Women (AAUW) Educational Foundation

May S (1994) *Women's experiences as distance learners: Access and technology, Journal of Distance Education.* Vol 9, no 1, pps 81-98.

Rogers A (1999) *Adult Education*. Ranslation: Papadopolou K. M. and Tobrou M, Metaixmio Publications, Athens.

Stalker J (1997) Women's participation in tertiary education: Misogynistic responses' in Crossing Borders, Breaking Boundaries: Research in the Education of Adults. Proceedings of the 27th Annual SCUTREA Conference.

United Nations (2000) Special Conference at the General Assembly, Women 2000: Equality between the sexes, Development and Peace for the 21st Century, New York, 5-9 June 2000. Action for the Equality of the Sexes and the Progress of Women.

Vergidis D (1995) *Undereducation: Social, Political and Cultural dimensions*. Epsilon Publications, 2nd edition.

10

Role and Performance of Kashmir Rural Development Department and Kashmir Humanity Foundation

Shakira S. Islam

Kashmir Rural Development Department, over the period of time, has assumed a key position in the socio-economic development of rural areas in view of the magnitude of funding provided by the Government of India and the State Government under various schemes. The Department aims at developing the rural economy in terms of infrastructure, creation of durable assets and generation of employment opportunities including creation of wage and self employment. It plays a vital role in upliftment of rural masses and has become an effective tool for reducing the number of people living below poverty line and also narrowing down the income inequalities between haves and the have-nots in rural sector.

Directorate of Rural Development, Kashmir comprises of 10 districts in Kashmir Valley and 2 districts in Ladakh region as given below:

Table 1:

S.No	*District*	*No. of Blocks*
01	Anantnag	7
02	Kulgam	5
03	Baramulla	12
04	Bandipora	5
05	Budgam	8
06	Kupwara	11
07	Pulwama	5
08	Shopian	1
09	Srinagar	1
10	Ganderbal	4
11	Leh	9
12	Kargil	9

Table 2: Schemes under Implementation in Rural Development Department, Kashmir

1.	Sampooran Gramin Rozgar Yojana (SGRY)
2.	National Rural Employment Guarantee Act (NREGA)
3.	Indira Awas Yojana (IAY)
4.	Rural Housing Scheme (RHS)
5.	Swranjayanti Gram Swarozgar Yojana (SGSY)
6.	Pradhan Mantri Gram SadakYojana (PMGSY)
7.	Model Villages (Prime Minister Re-construction Programme)
8.	Integrated Watershed Development Progamme (WDP Haryali)
9.	Finance Commission Award
10.	Prime Ministers Special Package

1. Sampoorna Gramin Rozgar Yojana (SGRY)

It was implemented in 2001. The scheme has following objectives:-

1) To provide additional wage employment in rural areas.
2) To provide food security.
3) To create durable community, social and economic infrastructure in rural areas.

4) Special emphasis to provide Wage Employment to:-

   a. Women

   b. Scheduled caste

   c. Scheduled Tribes.

   d. Parents of children withdrawn from hazardous occupations.

2. National Rural Employment Guarantee Scheme

The Parliament enacted an Act No. 42 of 2005 called the National Rural Employment Guarantee Act. The Act provides a guarantee for rural employment to house holds whose adult members volunteer to do un-skilled manual work not less than 100 days of such work in a financial year in accordance with the scheme made under the Act

The scheme:

- has been launched on February 2nd 2006 in 200 districts of the country. In J&K State it has been introduced in the Districts of Kupwara, Poonch and Doda in the first instance.
- is being extended to all other districts within 5 years in a phased manner.
- is expected to enhance people's livelihood on sustained basis by developing economic and social infrastructure in rural areas.
- is a direct attack on the causes of chronic poverty such as drought, deforestation and soil erosion.

This scheme is different from the earlier wage employment programmes in different ways:

(i) It provides legal guarantee of 100 days work to every rural household whose adult member volunteer to do un-skilled manual work.

(ii) If an applicant is not provided employment within 15 days he/she shall be entitled to unemployment allowance.

(iii) Rural Employment Guarantee Scheme is demand-driven instead of being supply-driven.

3. Indira Awas Yojna (IAY)

The scheme is designed to provide shelter to house-less people living in rural areas with special thrust on scheduled caste, scheduled tribe communities, freed bounded labourers and non-SC/ST families, living below poverty line. An amount of Rs. 25,500/- in plain areas and Rs. 27,500/- in hilly areas is provided by way of cash assistance in two installments to the beneficiaries. The funding pattern of the scheme between centre and State is 75: 25. The scheme is implemented through beneficiaries without the involvement of intermediaries. 3% of funds are earmarked for physically challenged persons. The guidelines of IAY programme have been modified to include up-gradation upto an amount of Rs. 12,500/- for unserviceable Kacha Houses in the rural areas and the scheme shall have now two components:

Construction of new houses 80% of allocation

Upgradation of unserviceable Kacha Houses 20% of allocation

4. Rural Housing Scheme (RHS)

The Rural Housing Scheme is a State plan scheme implemented in all the districts of Kashmir Division except District Leh. The scheme is implemented in accordance with the guidelines of IAY prescribed by the Ministry of Rural Development, Government of India.

5. Swranjayanti Gram Swarozgar Yojana (SGSY)

The Swranjayanti Gram Swarozgar Yojana was launched as an integrated programme for self-employment of the rural poor on 1st April 1999. The objective of the scheme is to bring the assisted poor families above the poverty line by organizing them into Self-Help Groups (SHGs) through the process of social mobilization, training, capacity building and provision of income generating assets through a mix of bank credit and Government subsidy. The funds are shared by State & Centre in the ratio of 25:75 and the eligible items of expenditure are as under:-

a) Training (10% of allocation)

b) Infrastructure (20% of allocation)

c) Revolving fund (10% of allocation)

d) Subsidy for economic activities (60% of allocation)

6. Pradhan Mantri Gram Sadak Yojana (PMGSY)

Objectives are:

1. To provide all weather roads to unconnected habitations having population more than 500.
2. New Roads - primary focus
3. Programme for Village Roads and Other District Roads only
4. Roads to be surfaced with white Topping

Many projects are already completed under Phase – I. Under Phase – II 45 Projects stand approved and the work on these projects is in full swing.

7. Model Village

The Hon'ble Prime Minister of India during his visit to Valley in October, 2004 announced Reconstruction programme for J&K State which included overall development of one village in each block as a model village by way of creating necessary infrastructure so as to change the outlook of villages and it serves as an example for carrying out developmental activities in other nearby villages in a phased manner.

The main objectives are:

* to minimize the Rural-Urban divide.
* Check the migration of population.
* Improve the quality of rural life.
* Demonstration of latest technology.
* Integrated development of area, based on local resources.

* Optimum utilization of resources available under various schemes.

8. Hariyali (IWDP)

The scheme was launched on 27th January 2003

Objectives are:

- Harvesting every drop of rainwater for purposes of irrigation, plantations including horticulture and floriculture, pasture development, fisheries etc. to create sustainable sources of income for the village community as well as for drinking water supplies.
- Ensuring overall development of rural areas through the Gram Panchayats and creating regular sources of income for the Panchayats from rainwater harvesting and management.
- Employment generation, poverty alleviation, community empowerment and development of human and other economic resources of the rural areas.
- Mitigating the adverse effects of extreme climatic conditions such as drought and desertification on crops, human and livestock population for the overall improvement of rural areas.
- Restoring ecological balance by harnessing, conserving and developing natural resources i.e. land, water, vegetative cover especially plantations.
- Encouraging village community towards sustained community action for the operation and maintenance of assets created and further development of the potential of the natural resources in the watershed.

Promoting use of simple, easy and affordable technological solutions and institutional arrangements that make use of, and build upon, local technical knowledge and available materials.

9. Finance Commission Awards

Finance Commission Awards is a centrally sponsored

scheme being implemented by the Rural Development Department. The main objective of the scheme till the completion of 11th FC Award period was to construct Panchayat Ghars for each Panchayat Halqa. However, the strategy has been changed under the 12th FC Award proposal under which it is envisaged to modernize and upgrade the standards of administration in terms of making the Panchayati Institutions functional by paying honorarium to the elected representatives, providing of trucks and road rollers for achieving quick and better quality results.

10. Prime Ministers Special Package (SGRY Additional)

The Prime Minister of India sanctioned a special package for J&K State in the year 2003-04 under which an allocation of Rs. 4.00 lacs were approved for each Panchayat Halqa (Rs. 3.00 lacs as Central Share and Rs. 1.00 lacs as State Share). Under the package, certain activities like construction of Community Information Centers, Food Godowns, Panchayat Ghars and school buildings etc. had to be undertaken. The scheme was implemented in accordance with the guidelines of SGRY.

Thus, there are a number of programmes for the development of the rural areas. As we all know, development of rural sector is inevitable for the overall development of our country. However, to get the results of the government sponsored rural development programmes, effective implementation plans are necessary by the concerned authorities. Despite the numerous promises and provisions made by the Indian government, the condition of poor people of the country continues to be pitiable. One of the ways to ensure effective implementation of these programmes is to involve good NGO's, which are already known for their good work and have earned the trust of the people.

In Kashmir, one such NGO is Kashmir Humanity Foundation (KHF). Kashmir Humanity Foundation is a well-recognized non-governmental organization (NGO) in Kashmir. In last year, its activities have broadened in the fields of female literacy, formal education for children, non-formal education, rural employment, income generating skills, community health and awareness programmes on various social issues.

Table 3: Some of the Development programmes takenup by KHF are:

Contruction of Primary School Building in a village	Sponsor Primary School Teaching Aids
Maruti Van For School children	Maruti Van for Mobile Health Clinic for far -flung villages
Cutting and Tailoring Centre/sewing class	Sponsor Embriodery Centre for poor girls
Sponsor Reading rooms for remote villages	Sponsor Candle Making Training centre for unemployed youths
Sponsor Agriculture Assistance centre to poor farmers	Sponsor Awareness Programs Like Aids, Dowry, Cancer Etc. in rural areas.
Adopt a village	Sponsorship for fisheries
Sponsor Fishers Net	Sponsor Cycle for news paper seller
Sponsor welding, scooter/ bike repairing, etc. training	Rehabilitation of Orphans
Preparatory school	Self help units/groups

Now, I would like to share some of my interesting experiences in rural part of Kashmir. This trip was arranged by the Kashmir University on the 31st July, 2009.

Roof Cultivation

The photograph - 1 shows roof cultivation in Gulmarg village. The soil in some villages of Kashmir is full of rocks and not suitable for cultivation. They put layers of soil with manure on the roof and cultivate there to get required good crops.

Gulmarg is connected by ropeway (gondola). It was written there that Gulmarg gondola is the world's longest ropeway. The ropeway with the cable – cabin can be seen on the left hand side in the photograph. From one such cable – cabin this photograph was taken.

We arrived at the last Gondola station (photograph – 2). It is a valley with one small peak in the Himalaya. It was partly covered by ice but there was no snow during our visit. Local people welcome tourist here. They run a mobile market and sell beautiful Kashmiri embroidered clothes and other items both for ladies and gents at reasonable prices. They also provide horse and sledge to tourist. These are the means of their living. Tourism is an important source of income in Kashmir.

Water Cultivation

The photographs (3, 4, 5) show water cultivation. They grow vegetables like pumpkins, beans, tomatoes, cucumbers etc.on the surface of water. The lady is collecting vegetables from her water garden in her boat. There are different owners of these water gardens. The water content of these vegetables is more than the vegetables grown on soil.

There are varieties of water lilies and also lotus in Kashmir. They use them for different purposes. Some variety they eat. The stem of water lily is very strong and looks like a rubber tube. The leaves are used as manure. In the photograph (4) the lady is collecting leaves of water lily in her boat. This photograph was taken from a shikara (decorative boat with cushion and curtain, shown in many movies). The shikara is a means of living to many Kashmiri families.

Ladies rowing their boats symbolizes women empowerment in rural India. This is observed in many other parts of India including Meghalaya. We also saw beautiful Chinars (Maple trees are also available in Canada, Maple leaf is used as an emblem of Canada), apple garden and strawberry garden.

(1)

(2)

(3)

(4)

(5)

(6)

REFERENCES

1. Directorate of Rural Development Kashmir: www.dr dk.nic.in
2. Government of Jammu and Kashmir, Department of Rural development: www.jkrd.nic.in

   Kashmir Humanity Foundation www.khblive.org

11

Indigenous People and Self-Determined Development

Victoria Tauli Corpuz

After the UN Declaration on the Rights of Indigenous People has been adopted by the General Assembly in 2007, suddenly many institutions like the UN institutions are pressurized to really look into how they have addressed the issues of indigenous peoples and of course we who know what has happened in history, we know very well that the UN hasn't really played a very good role in terms of the whole issue of development. The UN which is basically an organization of states has also been pursuing the dominant development model or the development paradigm of economic growth and then neo-liberal economies which basically pushes the whole idea that the market knows best and the government has to play a very low profile in terms of pushing for development and for many indigenous people all over the world, it is really the issue of the wrong kind of development that has pushed many of these people to protest and resist about what is happening in their own communities. In our own history, among the indigenous people in the northern parts of the Phillipines, we actually started strengthening our own movements because we suddenly found out that these developmental projects or the so called development projects like the Big Hydro electric Dams are becoming the major problems for the indigenous people.

During the period of the Maoist Dictatorship in the 60s upto the 70s they were just going around to our communities and one day we just discovered that there were helicopters hovering over our communities and some surveyors coming around. We wandered what they were doing in our community. We have never seen them before and that's when we only knew that there is such a thing called as the Chiko River Hydro electric dam which was already planned by the government and they were coming into our community just about to implement it without even asking us whether we would like to have that kind of project in our community and I think that's a common experience of indigenous people everywhere because at that time I remembered I was still in the first year in college. At the same time the whole issue of the Colorado Forest Highway in Brazil was implemented. This huge highway is going through the Amazon and indigenous peoples were protesting against it. This was also funded by the World Bank; this leads to protests by the Brazilian Amazon indigenous people and the people of Igorot against the Chiko River Dam. The protests are because of the reasons that the World Bank has not developed a policy for indigenous peoples, and thus, this was forced to withdraw the funding. The World Bank then decided that the loans sanctioned must be converted for development and safe guard policy for the indigenous people. To be fair to the World Bank that it was the first institution to develop a safe guard policy for protecting the indigenous peoples in the conduct of developmental work. This was the common history of many indigenous people all over the world, in fact in the Phillipines we called it the development aggression because it is really the way human rights are violated because of the so called developmental projects and that's the reason why we actually went to the UN. Due to this reason why many of our leaders were arrested or were arbitrarily put in jail and the key leader was assassinated.

We were wondering where we will go if we have a

dictatorship, there is nobody that we can address about this, and that is the time we heard that there was such a thing called as the Universal Declaration of Human Rights. We did not know about that before and this Declaration says that you cannot be arrested and tortured and then we realize that there is a body within the UN which was actually being set up to address indigenous people. Of course, this was initiated by the native Americans in the United States and Canada the Asami in Europe and the Aborigines in Australia. The only two groups of Asian indigenous peoples that actually attended the first meeting in 1982 were the Igorots from our organisation and the Chakma from the Chittagong Hill tracts in Bangladesh. They were the only two Asians who attended the UN Declaration and since then we started looking at the UN to really develop an instrument that will protect our rights against such kind of developmental projects first of all and off course what is more important is to really pushed the international community to recognized the collective rights of indigenous peoples to their lands, to their territories and resources. This is how all these indigenous movements have really gelled together and thus the UN provided us that space to be able to go there and link up with each other and share the progress and at the same time pushed the governments to develop international norms or standards that will protect us in our own communities. When we started doing that work, then we realize the amount of work, the amount of violation, the amount of gross violations that is happening all over the world and we persisted in pushing for this. It took almost 23 years for us to have this Declaration adopted which is really a long time, I mean most of my years is spent in pushing for this and I think this is worthwhile at the end. At present all the different UN institutions have pushed forward to implement this and the governments are also obliged to implement it. The last Articles 41 and 42 of the Declaration say that the UN agencies, its institutions and bodies have to effectively implement the Declaration and the UN Permanent Forum on Indigenous Peoples, the body that I am chairing now is also one of these bodies that have been ensured to monitor its effective implementation. Ofcourse the main duty holder to implement this Declaration is the United States and in the declaration the most important article and the most difficult article to negotiate was the Article 3 which was the article on the right to self determination. This article says that the indigenous peoples have the right to self determination and by virtue of that right they can freely determine their political status and they can determine how to carry out their economic, social and cultural development. So these points about the political status, this is something that the states cannot agree with. They thought how the indigenous people can determine what their political status is because basically what they think is that giving them their political status. Hence this Article states us to become independent or autonomous and that is the right which is being given to you.

The indigenous people have persisted to argue that in the declaration of the UN instruments in the UN civil and political rights and in the UN convention on economic and social rights, the Article 1 of this convention says about the right to self determination and if you look at the article it is exactly the same article as this one except there is no mention for indigenous people. It says that all peoples have the right to self determination, it is the people who have the rights and it is not the states that have the rights. The reason why there is such a thing as international law or international standard is because at the national level most of these are not implemented and the violation of the rights of the people is really done at the national level. If there is no international law that sets a standard on how states should behave towards their own citizens then these people will have no chance to redress or obtain justice for what the state has been doing to them. So that's the reason why we have an international law, if you are going to qualify it by saying based on national circumstances then you're effectively undermining the essence of what an international human rights law. We have to sharpen our experience in debating with the states against the lawyers of the states. We sharpen all these arguments and eventually won and that is one of the biggest victories of indigenous people and off course the most important article on self determination is Article 26 which is on the right to the lands, territories, resources which says that the indigenous peoples have rights to control, own and manage their lands, territories and resources and they have the right to determine how to manage and how to make these lands productive for themselves.

There is another article, an Article 32 which says that the indigenous peoples have the right to development and the states should obtain free prior and inform consent of indigenous people before any development projects is brought into their community. So free prior and inform consent is one of the principles that is enshrined in the declaration and you can see if you have a chance to read the declaration. There are six articles talking about free prior and inform consent. This is also one of the things that many of the states refused to put in the declaration. The US especially protests against the free prior and inform consent and even now in the recent Climate Change Negotiations where Phrang and I were two weeks ago in Bangkok. We manage to put a phrase, an agreement saying that indigenous peoples and their free prior inform consent should be obtained before any policies on forest and climate change are being designed, implemented and monitored. The US totally refused, saying that "There is no way that we are going to agree to that phrase on free and prior consent" and I said "well that is what is contained in the UN declaration. Well we did not vote for the declaration because there are four countries who voted against the adaptation of the Declaration and that is the US, New Zealand, Canada and Australia". So these are the four countries who voted against it and they are the ones who are persistently voting against the reference to free prior and inform consent in the Climate Change Negotiations. So that is the situation we find ourselves in, but off course in spite of all this we are in a situation where we have really raised the level of awareness of many indigenous people in various parts of the world.

There are several Indigenous Peoples Movements in different countries of the world. We have really influence significantly various decisions that are being made internationally. Just recently the International Fund for Agriculture and Development (IFAD) in which Kyrham and I are members of the board, they passed a policy on indigenous people. In the past during Phrang's time we have a difficult time pushing for this because they say why should we have a policy for indigenous people because they are related to rural development and we said what about poverty, about marginality of indigenous peoples. In rural areas majority of the indigenous peoples are inhabited, they are the ones who are discriminated against their rights so you have to have a policy and eventually a month ago the Board agreed to have a policy made. The other thing which we succeeded is the UNDG, the UN has developed various issues in bodies like the ILO the FAO, WHO are all under this umbrella. Last year they finally passed the UNDG Guidelines on Indigenous Peoples Issues which means that all the countries who teamed up with various UN bodies should implement these guidelines. The World Bank recently revised their indigenous people's policy and now they have adopted by saying no to Free Prior Inform Consent but as the Free Prior Inform Consultation. Finally, an agreement is brought for the indigenous people since they hate the word Consent, because they say that the word consent means they have the right to say no and we say off course that what consent is about. You can either say no or yes and that's the only thing you can do and so they did away with the word. Since the US being the major contributor and stock holder of the bank it succeeded in ostracizing against that kind of objectives so this is the main challenge that we facing.

The global context now is in a total different situation where we are met with the most serious prices that we can ever see in our life time. The first of course is the climate change crisis which provides an evidence of how development has failed because of the industrial type of development that is the development that the west has promoted increasing green house gases emission. About 80 percent of the green house gases emissions that we are having now actually comes from the historical emissions of the United States which has 5 percent of the World's population and now they are asking the developing countries to cut back on their emissions but in the atmosphere there is almost no space left for the developing countries to have their emissions because they too have to develop, and since the industrial revolution the developing nations have develop at a pace so unprecedented that they have polluted the atmosphere to a level where we are facing all the worst impacts of climate change like floods, droughts, the melting of glaciers, health problems, etc. The WHO came up with a report saying that the increase in malaria, dengue has increased tremendously since they have a direct link with global warming. Destruction of forest are caused by the climate change because if the temperature would go so high resulting in bush fires. Our counterpart that is the North American Canadian native particularly the indigenous people say that in the temperate forest they have spruce beetles and during winter these beetles would die and the forest will regenerate again but now because the temperature has increase the spruce beetle continue to live for more months and now many of the forest are disappearing because the temperature has risen significantly. So all the problems that we are facing with climate change is really the strongest evidence to say that we cannot continue to do development in the same way that development has been happening in the past two hundred years. We really have to shift towards a low carbon growth. However indigenous people are saying that we never contributed to this problem but in fact most of our indigenous economies, systems, agricultural systems, and forest management systems are carbon neutral. We have the smallest carbon foot print in the world and yet now we are being look upon to provide the solution. Our forest are suddenly part of the solution because they discover that 20 percent of green house gases emissions are coming from tropical rain forest so now they are saying we should give incentive to the tropical rain forest countries having rich tropical forest so that they will not cut their forest. So that means they will quest again our forest and you are not allowed to do anything with these forest because they are carbon fixed and you cannot disturbed the forest. There is a great danger here because of this solution and they are going to exclude us again or they will violate our rights to our forest so that is one of the big fights that we have in the climate change negotiations.

The rights of indigenous peoples to their forest should be recognizing before you even think of any forest and climate change mitigation measure. Everything they have to develop the renewable sources of energy and renewable means hydro electric dams since they consider this renewable energy sources and off course what do we have? Most of the high rivers are found in the indigenous territories where in North East India only there are around 100 dams which are covered in the blue print of your energy programmes and most of those are here and more than 100 I think are in NE India. Another thing of course is the bio fuel plantations; they would like to plant more oil palm, more jatropha in the lands remaining lands because these are sources of bio fuels to feed the cars of the rich people in the rich countries. These solutions have suffered the most from the impacts of climate change; even the solutions that are being talked off are also going to impact on us. Nuclear power plant, now the nuclear industry is so busy lobbying the climate change convention to include nuclear power as a renewable energy or as a clean energy, so that is why you are having all these plans to mined uranium in your region because nuclear now is going to have a good image because it's a clean energy . Again where are they getting this uranium they are getting in indigenous territories but the worst thing is that the radioactive waste that comes from these plants are going to be dump in indigenous territories. This is the problem being faced now by the American Indians in the US because many of the radioactive wastes are being dumped in their communities and because they are so poor the government is willing to give them a little money as a payment for dumping the waste in their communities which is really a very tragic situation for most of our counterparts in that place. So this is the situation with this climate change problem on the one hand it is a problem that is being created by the wealthy countries, the wealthy people and on the other hand it is going to be the poor people in the poor countries who are going to provide the solution for them and the commitments in terms of giving money, finance to the developing countries to be able to mitigate and adapt and in terms of providing technologies so that we will be able to develop low anti pollution devices all these technologies that will really lower green house gases emissions. They are not providing that they are not adhering to their responsibilities. So there is a great amount of work that needs to be done for the world to pressure these rich countries to adhere to their obligations not only under international human rights law but also underdevelopment under the whole issue of development and the whole issue of climate change. They are obliged by international agreements to provide to developing countries 0.7 percent of their GDP to the developing countries as official aid. None of those countries are adhering to that now when they are having this global economic crisis which is of their own making they can easily give 3 trillion dollars to bail out the richest companies, their banks and their financial houses and yet they cannot even provide 100 billion for the climate change convention to be able to do mitigation for developing countries. So that is the dilemma in the whole climate change negotiations and its going to collapse even before it reaches Copenhagen because of the refusal of the US. To be fair to India in the last negotiations they were the ones who were fighting strongly against the US and Europe because they didn't like to have to meet their obligations. They wanted to kill the Kyoto Protocol which is the protocol that sets the target for them and that sets the target in terms of lowering their emissions but also in terms of finance and technology. Now they wanted to kill the whole protocol because they wanted to bring on board the US as it was not part of the Kyoto Protocol and to come up with a new one which will include the US. That's what they say, but the Kyoto protocol was adapted in 1997 it only came into effect in 2005 so if we are going to develop a protocol by December maybe it will come into effect in 2020 and by that time we are all dead because of all the disasters that we are facing so this is the kind of world that we have so in that kind of situation the contributions of indigenous people all over the world is really going to be vital because:

Most of the lands, most of the forest, the tropical rain forest that is in the world today are actually found in indigenous territories. From the findings scientist say that the tropical forest are keeping under them and within the trees about 4.8 gigatons of carbon dioxide which is twice the amount of green house gases emissions in the atmosphere so if you are going to deforest these forest you will release all this carbon which is kept under the ground and that is going to cause a major disaster. So they need our forest very badly so what we need to do is to really use this opportunity to change the laws of the land if this country is to really recognize our rights to control our forest but also to recognize our traditional forest management practices because that is the main reason why this forest is still there because we have been fighting to have control over this forest and also to continue practicing our own forest management practices.

Now in terms of traditional knowledge, they also found out that in terms of adapting to climate change indigenous people have develop varieties of crops that can withstand floods, even droughts we have develop different system like water systems, water management systems that ensure that we can still continue to have some water in our communities. They know and have discovered that we have knowledge over traditional medicines, but now the move is not to help reinforce us to continue doing this but to grab and actually steal this knowledge by claiming intellectual property rights over this kind of knowledge. So we have to continue to fight for the protection of our traditional knowledge and to really be identified. Given the incentive to reinforce strength and even upscale the use of this knowledge we will continue this kind of knowledge to the dominant society why not. That is what we have been doing anyway since time immemorial. We easily share our knowledge but this ownership and the recognition where this knowledge comes from should not be shifted to the private corporations who are just so eager to get it because they know they will earn more profit from doing that. So that is the other issue on how to ensure that our traditional system of burning the forest can be protected.

Traditional agricultural systems like shifting cultivation can still be protected. They have demonized shifting cultivation so much saying that this is the major cause of deforestation etc, etc. But now there are more and more studies coming up but actually shifting cultivation if done in the way that indigenous people are doing they regenerate the forest, they strengthen the soils in the forest etc. We have to come up with studies and more evidences to show that these kind of practices are actually carbon neutral and they are going to contribute in a low carbon kind of society. So these are only a few of the things that we should put in our own development, self determined development paradigm but off course for us to be able to do that we really have to ensure that governance mechanism are also put into place. Now for instance if they are going to provide incentives like money for us to keep our forest standing, what kinds of laws that should be put into place at the national level that will really protect our rights to our forest. Secondly what kinds of governance mechanism are we going to put into place so that the money that will come in is not going to end up in the pockets of politicians because forest area is where you noticed the highest number of corruption is happening. So if we don't put governance mechanism that will really ensure that kind of accountability and transparency then we'll end up in the same situation where the politicians will get all the money and the indigenous people who have been protecting this, will just end up without anything. So those are the kind of processes that we'll have to put into place the governance mechanisms, the laws that will protect us and of course the adaptation of the Human Rights Based Approach to

Development. So this is a very important approach because as we have seen development usually violates human rights and to ensure that when development takes place, the Human Rights of peoples are not violated, the Human Rights Approach is already really very well developed and the UN Declaration on the Rights of Indigenous People is a key Framework for that kind of Approach and finally the Ecosystem Approach. Indigenous People all over the world have really been the ones with the best ecosystem managers in the world because we look at the whole system in a holistic way, we have to think of the forest, the water etc. we always have that kind of ethics or worldly view that everything is related to everythingp. Even our relations with nature is very much rare in place so if we are able to really reclaim, revive and strengthen our ecosystem our point of view will be strengthen to influence many of the approaches to development and of course the climate change processes. Then there will be the chance that we can strengthen our development in a friendlier environment approach. So these are just a few elements of what we mean when we say self determined development and there are still much more to be done. I like to say that it is a challenge for all of us how do we gather all this good practices that are happening in different countries in terms of managing ecosystems, managing in terms of developing governance systems that are more democratic and more transparent and accountable in terms of ensuring that we have a fair share of what is generated from all this whole issue of benefit sharing in terms of protecting our rights to our land and resources and our rights to continue practicing our cultures and to protect our biodiversity. So these are just few of the elements of what we mean when we talk about self determined development and its going to be a huge challenge because now with the economic crisis again they are trying to reinvent ways, doing things and they will be replicating some of the things that we have been talking about maybe defining it in a way that will favour their own interest and that is what we have to be very conscious about. How do we make sure that they will not co-op the land wage concept and used it in a way that is going to be working against our own interest. I think many of you who are academicians have a task to play, in terms of participating in this kind of debate, participating in designing that kind of development that the world needs badly and participating in decisions making to influence the decisions that are going to be made by the politicians in our country and also the global community. These are the challenges that we all face now and I know we can do it because we have shown now that we are able to influence many of the international decisions. The Climate Change Negotiations now never in their history we can see a reference to the indigenous people but now in the documents being written whether it is adaptation, mitigation , the issue of forest and climate change, the issue of technology transfer, there are all references to indigenous people in the document . The secretary of the Global Issue on Indigenous People last week in Bangkok he says "oh I'm so impressed with all of you for the first time that there are all these references to indigenous people, you are the most organized group in the whole meeting and have been able to bring in your own interest into the Declaration and many of the governments are now saying indigenous people. Even India said when i spoke because I said you cannot talk of forest without talking of the collective Rights of Indigenous People which is contained in the UN Declaration on the Rights of Indigenous People. This is the reason why we are insisting that will be put there and India said we support what the Phillippines said. So that's a good sign that we can led India to say Indigenous Peoples because in the past they say all of us are indigenous, so now they are saying we do understand the contributions that indigenous people can make. Of course other forest dwelling people will agree because we always say indigenous people in our local communities. So now we are in that kind of situation where we should grab that opportunity and seize the opportunity with that kind of openness to really accommodate our own views and perspectives and in terms of how development should happen.

I'm challenging all of you now whether you are politicians, academics, students or whatever you do that this is the approached that you should seized and I think here in India you have that kind of space. I hope you will be able to use it significantly because India has now become a major player in all the negotiations happening over the world today so if you are able to change the way India thinks and at the global level will be able to put that kind of pressure then the leaders hope that we'll be able to see some changes in the near future.

Index

****